JESUS IS COMING: 500 ILLUSTRATIONS

JESUS IS COMING:
500 ILLUSTRATIONS

by
PAUL LEE TAN, Th.D.

ASSURANCE PUBLISHERS
P.O. Box 684
Rockville, Maryland 20853

JESUS IS COMING: 500 ILLUSTRATIONS
Copyright © 1978
Paul Lee Tan

Library of Congress Catalog Card Number: 78-73219
International Standard Book Number: 0-932940-03-X

PRINTED IN THE UNITED STATES OF AMERICA

To
**Our Dear Little
Christine and Stephen**

From Affectionate Parents

Preface

Everyone appreciates a good illustration. The right illustration at the right time is half the battle for many preachers and teachers. Congregations have come to life, tears, or wholesome laughter, at an illustration fittingly given. Sunday School and Bible classes have become enthusiastic learning centers where wise usage of illustrative materials is employed. Even in the study, the discovery of a good illustration has opened up new avenues of thought and conviction for many a speaker.

Having been involved in the preaching and teaching ministries of the church for some two decades, I have experientially known the needs of active Christian workers for heart-stirring illustrations. I have found that a message normally requires 3-4 illustrations, or 20-30 short, pithy allusions. And the trend is for more short illustrations, rather than a few long stories. In fact, a Christian worker will need at least some 20 new illustrations each *week* for use in various services of the church.

In selecting materials for the book, a conscientious effort has been made to exclude what is irrelevant, repetitious, trite and hackneyed, archaic, mythical, profane and impious. The reader will also note an absence of prosaic applications, personal conclusions, and redundant explanations. All illustrations are purposely kept factual, brief and to the point—without undue moralizing and pious applications.

Because of this self-imposed restraint, over twice as much factual material is possible. The reader should be able to get to the point at once, and make necessary applications from the slant of the telling, its classfication, as well as the Scripture references given.

Many of the selections in this volume come from personal experiences and writings. Many others have been adapted from newspaper and magazine sources, culled from books, plucked from the lips of public speakers, and (a few) drawn from the imagination. I have tried to give credit whenever possible. Illustrations however are so often heard, read, seen, copied, adapted, concised, reworded, applied, dreamed out and made out that it is frequently hard to go to "first" source. Nevertheless, continual effort is being made to locate sources, and to incorporate in a later printing.

Topics in Book. The topics in the book are selected and arranged according to the various "signs" of the Lord's coming. The convenient alphabetical arrangements of the 500 illustrations under 100 "signs" (topics) is the result of much care and thought.

In most instances, classification is according to the slant or emphasis of the narration. Thus, an illustration may illustrate several points, but according to how it is told or applied, I have classified it under one main topic. In other cases, several topics have been grouped together, since experience shows that it is less time-consuming to glance through one major topic than to look for similar topics spread out under different sections of a big book. Thus, *Preachers* would cover ministers, clergy, preaching, etc., and *Family* embraces home, houses, etc. A generous amount of cross-references guide one to these major topics in the book and to other related topics.

The Index. If the 100 topics in the body of the book should be insufficient, the detailed *Index* at the end of the book will come to the rescue. The reader should early get acquainted with the *Index* and use it profusely. It has been carefully arranged for maximum success in searching for or recalling an illustration. With practice, one should be able to turn to a subject and find an apt illustration with ease and speed.

This volume has another theme: the coming of Christ. The various "signs" of our Lord's coming are arranged alphabetically in the body of the book. We will note that while the "signs" occurring today are severe enough, they are nothing compared to *actual* occurrences at the Great Tribulation. The things in this book are mere foreshadowings. The real things are yet to come!

Conclusion. Evangelical teachers and preachers, standing apart from ritualistic religion, must speak with down-to-earth clarity on the things of God. Since few tools open the "windows" of sermons like apt illustrations, Christian workers have gladly spent time in search for good illustrative materials.

This volume is a compendium from another book—*Signs of The Times: 7,700 Illustrations.* The reader will ultimately want to get this larger volume, which contains ten times as much choice illustrative materials.

As this book goes its way into the hands and hearts of Christian workers everywhere, it is my prayer that our Lord will bless it to the spiritual edification of many before He comes.

P.L. Tan

CONTENTS

Contents

ALCOHOLISM

1 Alcoholism's Cost to Society

Altogether, alcoholism now is said to be costing society around $25 billion annually. Of this, 10 billion dollars is lost by the nation's employers, because of absenteeism and low productivity of alcoholic personnel whose absentee rate is 2½ times as much as other workers.

Law officials estimate the cost for arrest, trial and jailing of drinkers at more than 100 million dollars yearly. Almost half the 5.5 million arrests annually in the US are related to alcoholic abuse.

2 Most Alcoholic Person

The most alcoholic person was in England. A person by the name of Vanhorn averaged over four bottles of ruby port daily for 23 years prior to his death at 61. He emptied 35,688 bottles in his lifetime.

3 A Drama That Drowned

Ecarte, a play presented in London about 1875, holds the record for having the shortest run in the history of the theatre. At the end of the first act on the opening night, the producer, disgusted with himself and his company, informed the audience that the play would not continue, refunded the money and closed the house for the rest of the season. Having been in a generous mood before the curtain arose on this scene, in which considerable drinking took place, the producer had ordered real champagne served and, consequently, the players were "finished" before the act.

—Freling Foster

4 Two Most Costly Drinks

On the last day of Lincoln's life, the great emancipator said: "We have cleared up a colossal job. Slavery is abolished. After reconstruction the next great question will be the overthrow and suppression of the legalized liquor traffic."

That evening, Mr. Booth stopped in a saloon, filled himself with liquor to nerve himself for his planned tragedy. That night Lincoln's bodyguard left the theater for a drink of liquor at the same saloon. While he was away Booth shot Lincoln. Those two drinks were the most costly drinks in American history.

—Selected

17

ANGELS

5 Billy Graham On Angels

Billy Graham says: "As an evangelist, I have often felt too far spent to minister from the pulpit to men and women who have filled stadiums to hear a message from the Lord. Yet again and again my weakness has vanished, and my strength has been renewed. I have been filled with God's power not only in my soul but physically. On many occasions, God has become especially real, and has sent His unseen angelic visitors to touch my body to let me be His messenger for heaven, speaking as a dying man to dying men."

6 Large Audience Of Angels

An old minister worked into the night on a sermon for his small congregation. His unsympathetic wife chided him for spending so much time on a message that so few will appreciate. To this the minister replied: "You forget, my dear, how large my audience will be!" If angels are looking, nothing on earth done for Christ is trivial.

ANGER

7 High Cost Of Anger

Anger weakens a man. It puts him at a disadvantage in every undertaking in life. When Sinbad and his sailors landed on one of their tropical islands, they saw high up in the trees coconuts which could quench their thirst and satisfy their hunger. The coconuts were far above the reach of Sinbad and the sailors, but in the branches of the trees were the chattering apes. Sinbad and his men began to throw stones and sticks up at the apes. This enraged the monkeys and they began to seize the coconuts and hurl them down at the men on the ground. That was just what Sinbad and his men wanted. They got the apes angry so that the apes would gather their food for them. That is a good illustration of how by indulgence in anger we play into the hands of our foes.

—C. E. Macartney

8 The Echo

I shouted aloud and louder
While out on the plain one day;
The sound grew faint and fainter
Until it had died away.
My words had gone forever.
They left no trace or track,
But the hills nearby caught up the cry
And sent an echo back.

I spoke a word in anger
To one who was my friend,
Like a knife it cut him deeply,
A wound that was hard to mend.
That word, so thoughtlessly uttered,
I would we could both forget,
But its echo lives and memory gives
The recollection yet.

How many hearts are broken,
How many friends are lost
By some unkind word spoken
Before we count the cost!
But a word or deed of kindness
Will repay a hundredfold.
For it echoes again in the hearts of men
And carries a joy untold.

—C. A. Lufburrow

9 Caesar Reciting The Alphabet

It is said of Julius Caesar that, when provoked, he used to repeat the whole Roman alphabet before he allowed himself to speak.

10 Epigram

●The greatest remedy for anger is delay.   —Seneca

●The best answer to anger is silence.
—German Proverb

●Keep cool; anger is not an argument.
—Daniel Webster

●Swallowing angry words before you say them is better than having to eat them afterwards.

●"He who goes to bed angry has the devil for a bed-fellow." Never take your enemies to bed with you.
—Old Latin

ANTICHRIST

11 Names Of The Antichrist

The name of the Antichrist is not given to us in Scripture. But some Bible writers have definite terms used of him, as follows:

Assyrian—Isa. 10:5
Beast—Rev. 13:1
Chaldean—Hab. 1:6
King of Fierce Countenance
—Dan. 8:23
Little Horn—Dan. 7:8
Man of Sin—II Thess. 2:3
Son of Perdition—II Thess. 2:3
Vile Person—Dan. 11:21
The Wicked—II Thess. 2:8

12 Some Inconspicuous Beginnings

Antichrist will rise inconspicuously. Here are some interesting facts of history:

(1) At age 22. Alexander the Great was only a petty prince. But only four years later, he was Master of the known world and had radically changed the course of history.

(2) Napoleon Bonaparte was born on the 15th of August, 1769 at Ajaccio, Corsica. which was won to France by arms. Had the young man seen the light two months earlier, he would have been by birth an Italian, not a Frenchman.

(3) General Ulysses Grant would not have been a military man had it not been that his rival for a West Point cadetship had been found to have six toes on each foot instead of five.

(4) In a book published in 1933, Dorothy Thompson related that it took her just 50 seconds after meeting Adolf Hitler to decide that "that formless, almost faceless man" would never become the dictator of Germany.

13 Ancient Numbers Code

Many ancient languages did not have separate symbols which stand for numbers, as we do. Rather, the letters of the alphabet were used to designate numbers also. For instance, each letter of the Hebrew alphabet has a numerical value. This method of calculating a name by the use of numbers is known as "Gematria," practiced seriously by the Jews.

The following ancient number code could be used on any alphabetical language:

A-1	H-8	O-60	V-400
B-2	I-9	P-70	W-500
C-3	J-10	Q-80	X-600
D-4	K-20	R-90	Y-700
E-5	L-30	S-100	Z-800
F-6	M-40	T-200	
G-7	N-50	U-300	

14 "Any Person's Name Can Fit"

Professor Salmon said,

Any name, with sufficient ingenuity, can be made to yield the number 666. There are three rules by the help of which, I believe, an ingenious man could find the required sum in any given name. First, if the proper name by itself will not yield it; add a title; secondly, if the sum cannot be found in Greek, try Hebrew, or even Latin; thirdly, do not be too particular about the spelling. The use of a language different from that to which the name properly belongs allows a good deal of latitude in the transliteration.

APATHY

15 Where Are The Samaritans?

In New York City a mailman, shot by a sniper, is ordered from a building lobby because he is dripping blood.

In Oklahoma City a woman gives birth unexpectedly—on a city sidewalk. Bystanders turn their faces. A taxi driver looks, then speeds away. A nearby hotel refuses a blanket.

In Dayton, Ohio, a dozen people see a woman drive her car into the Miami River. They watch indifferently as the woman climbs on the car's roof and screams that she can't swim. The woman drowns.

So many incidents like this have happened that the Chicago Sun-Times library now has a special file tabbed "Apathy."

—James C. Hefley

16 Voting Power Of Saloon Keepers

A survey of voting habits in an area of Chicago some two decades ago showed:

99 percent of the tavern keepers voted.
97.5 percent of the gamblers and their employees voted.
16 percent of the housewives voted.
17 percent of the Protestant ministers voted.
29 percent of the Protestant laymen voted.

17 So What!

A teacher gave a subject for composition class. The subject given was "WHAT?" For an hour, the whole class busily elucidated, expanded, and defined this word and related concepts in pages of paper. A mischievous boy submitted his paper in 1 minute and left the class. On his sheet, he had written: "SO WHAT?"

APOSTASY

18 Apostasy Of Judson Memorial Church

In New York City there is a church built in honor of the great missionary to Burma Adoniram Judson, but apostasy has closed in on this church, and from what goes on there it has no right to be called a church. They put on a show on Flag Day—a show "dedicated to the stars and stripes." There were depraved and obscene exhibits, defiling the flag, and according to Max Geldman in the National Review, there were exhibits that were "simply unquotable." The police closed down the show, it was so rotten.

On another occasion the pews were removed to make room for dancing and the people sat in circles of folding chairs. The pulpit had been removed for a presentation of "Winnie the Pooh" and had not been replaced. The place where the choir used to be is vacant. On Sunday a nude couple danced there during the service. This "church" is so deep in the apostasy that it would have to reach up to touch bottom.

—Christian Victory

19 Stalin—A Saved Man?

In The Alliance Witness David Enlow quotes the "Red" Dean of Canterbury, Dr. Hewlett Johnson, as having made the statement: "Stalin was a rough and stern man . . . because he had a dirty job to do. But God's eye is a big eye and sees everything, good and bad. To know all is to forgive all. So from Heaven's point of view I think Stalin is safe."

20 Founding Purposes Of Early Colleges

Eighty-eight of the first 100 colleges founded in America were organized to promote the Gospel and the claims of Jesus Christ.

Every collegiate institution founded in the colonies prior to the Revolutionary War—except University of Pennsylvania—was establish by some branch of the Christian church.

Even at the University of Pennsylvania, the evangelist George Whitefield played a prominent part. The first building of the present university was build for the purpose of accommodating the crowds which wanted to hear Whitefield preach—a decision of Benjamin Franklin and other supporters. A statue of Whitefield stands on that campus today.

21 Harvard's Christ-Centered Rules

Harvard's "Rules and Precepts" (adopted in 1646), read:

(1) Every one shall consider the main end of his life and studies to know God and Jesus Christ which is eternal life.

(2) Seeing the Lord giveth wisdom, every one shall seriously by prayer in secret seek wisdom of him.

(3) Every one shall so exercise himself in reading the Scriptures twice a day that they be ready to give an account of their proficiency therein, both in theoretical observations of languages and logic, and in practical and spiritual truths . . . "

And thus, 52% of the 17th century Harvard graduates became ministers!

ARAB WEALTH

22 The World Of Oil

The Arab world occupies 8% of the globe, yet possesses nearly two-thirds of the world's total known supply of oil. The world's proven oil reserves are given as follows:

Western Europe	10.3 billion bbl.
Africa	15.3 billion bbl.
Southeast Asia	14.0 billion bbl.
South America	25.5 billion bbl.
North America	47.2 billion bbl.
Communist World . .	54.9 billion bbl.

ARAB WORLD . . . . 390.0 billion bbl.

23 Buying The United States

To illustrate the enormous amount of buying power being transferred to the 13 members of the Organization of Petroleum Exporting Countries (OPEC), here are some examples of what just one year's oil revenues, $125 billion billion, could buy or finance in the U.S.—

— The entire U. S. farm crop
— All the stocks in the 30 biggest industrial corporations
— All the steel produced in U.S. for 4½ years
— All the cars and trucks produced for 3½ years
— 10,000 F-5 fighter aircraft
— 3,200,000 private houses
— One fourth of the total U.S. Government debt
— Nearly all debt of local governments
— New York State's budget for 13 years
— All plant and equipment outlays for a year

ARMAGEDDON

24 Cockpit Of The World

Belgium is called "the cockpit of Europe" because it has been the site of more European battles than any other country—such as the battles of Oudernarde, Ramillies, Fontenoy, Fleurus, Jemmapes, Ligny, Waterloo, etc.

The plain of Megiddo was also the scene of many decisive battles in Israel's history. Here Gideon defeated Midian (Judg. 6:33). Here Saul died on Mount Gilboa (I Sam. 31:1). Here Josiah was slain against Pharoah-Nechoc (II Kg. 23:29,30).

Here also, battles have occurred between Egyptians and Assyrians, between Babylonians and Greeks, between Seleucids and Ptolemies, between Romans and Arabs, between Crusaders and Turks.

Napoleon called this area "the world's greatest natural battlefield" because of the ideal terrain for the world's armies to maneuver.

25 400 Million Casualties

The total number of soldiers to be at the Battle of Armageddon will come from at least the following two sources:

a. 200 million from Asia (Rev. 9:16);

b. 200 million from Antichrist's western forces.

Ten percent of the US population served in the armed forces during World War II. Ten percent of the present-day 4 billion world population would be 400 million in the armed forces at Armageddon. The result: 400 million casualties!

26 Boundaries Of Armageddon

"The battlefield stretches from Megiddo on the north (Zech. 12:11; Rev. 16:16) to Edom on the south (Isa. 34:5-6; 63:1), a distance of approximately 200 miles. It reaches from the Mediterranean sea on the west to the hills of Moab on the east, a distance of almost 100 miles.

It includes the valleys of Jehoshaphat (Joel 3:2,2) and the plains of Esdraelon. And the center of the entire area is the city of Jerusalem (Zech. 14:1-2).

The kings with their armies come from the north and the south, from the east and from the west. There is an invasion from hell beneath. And entering the scene at the last moment is an invasion from outer space."

—Herman A. Hoyt

ASCETICISM

27 Asceticism On A Rampage

During the fourth century, hundreds of ascetics sought to escape temptation and punish their bodies by living as hermits.

The extremes to which they went in their attempts to deny gratification of "physical lusts" seem incredible.

St. Ascepsimas wore so many chains that he had to crawl around on hands and knees. Besarion, a monk, would not even give in to his body's desire for restful sleep—for forty years he would not lie down while sleeping. Macarius the Younger sat naked in a swamp for six months until mosquito bites made him look like a victim of leprosy. St. Maron spent eleven years in a hollowed-out tree trunk. Others lived in caves, dens of beasts, dry wells—even tombs.

To suffer the discomfort of filth, stench, worms, and maggots were considered to be spiritually beneficial and a sign of victory over the body.

28 Perpetual Silence

In Westmael, near Antwerp, there is a convent of trappist monks who live under the vow of perpetual silence. They dress in rough sackcloth, their heads shaven and beards unkept. They sleep on hard boards and eat bread, sour milk and vegetables. Everyday, the monks goes to the garden to look into an open grave which awaits the first monk to die.

29 Wesley And Asceticism

Young John Wesley, before his conversion, anxiously sought rest for his soul, finally deciding on a solitary life in one of the Yorkshire dales. His wise mother interposed, saying that "God had better work for you to do."

Wesley travelled many miles to consult "a serious man." "The Bible knows nothing of a solitary religion," advised the good man.

Then, Wesley turned about and faced his career which was to make his personal history a part of the history of his country and Christianity.

ATHEISTS

30 University Of Atheism

In Ashkabad, the capital of Turkmenistan, near the USSR-Iranian border, is a newly opened University of Atheism. It is offering a six-month course to further the spread of scientific-atheistic knowledge. Graduates are expected to continue "the struggle against religion."

31 A Town Called "Liberal"

Few years ago, a group of people in Missouri founded a town and named it Liberal. They were so extremely 'liberal' that churches were not to be allowed. In their boom literature they boasted that it was 'the only town of its size in the United States without a priest, a preacher, church, God, Jesus, hell or devil.'

But Elder Clark Braden wrote up an account for the *Post Dispatch* showing that there was little else than hell and devil there, that it was a den of iniquity, that its hotels were brothels and virtue almost unknown. The account was so terrible that they had Braden arrested for criminal libel, and sued him and the *Post Dispatch* for $25,000 damages.

After the prosecution had presented all of its evidence, the case was submitted to the jury without rebutting evidence by the defendant and he was acquitted by the jury. The civil suit for damages was dismissed by demand of the plaintiffs, who paid all the costs.

Liberal was a failure, and even lifelong unbelievers, who had moved there for its advantages, left in disgust. One of them struck the keynote when he said: "An infidel surrounded by Christians may spout his infidelity and the community may be able to stand it but it will never do to establish a society with infidelity as its basis."

—*Ministers' Research Service*

32 Ingersoll Gives God Five Minutes

Robert Ingersoll, after delivering one of his addresses, pulled his watch from his pocket and said, "According to the Bible, God has struck men to death for blasphemy. I will blaspheme Him and give Him five minutes to strike me dead and damn my soul."

There was a period of perfect silence while one minute went by; two minutes passed, and people began to get nervous; three minutes, and a woman fainted; four minutes, and Ingersoll curled his lip.

At five minutes, he snapped shut his watch, put it in his pocket, and said: "You see, there is no God, or He would have taken me at my word."

The story was told later to Joseph Parker, who said, "And did the American gentleman think he could exhaust the patience of God in five minutes?"

—H. A. Ironside

33 Atheist's Daring Challenge Came True

Gerald B. Winrod, who was editor of *The Defender*, related a remarkable story about an atheist who had been very bold, blatant and outspoken against God and the Bible. He had defied God by saying, "If there is a God, my grave will be infested with snakes."

At the funeral it was necessary to remove a snake from the grave before the coffin could be lowered, the sexton saying that he had killed four big snakes at one time, yet never saw a snake at any other grave.

Mr. Winrod's informant said he would ask a gentleman in Ohio to give him more details, and in due course he received a further word, together with a picture of the bronze monument of the atheist, Chester Beddell, who had died in 1908 at the age of 82.

The letter said, "Mr. Beddell said while living there was no God, and he never did believe in one. He did not hesitate to

23

speak of these things .... He built the monument years before his death. His statue is of bronze. and in his uplifted right hand there is a scroll with this inscription. 'Universal Mental Liberty'. Under his left foot is a scroll representing the Bible. with the inscription. 'Superstition'. Before his death he made this remark: 'If there is a God, or any truth in the Bible. let my body be infested with snakes'.

"Since his burial the family lot has been full of snake holes around the curbing. Snakes can be seen any day you visit the graveyard. Last year twenty of us went out on the 30th October. and saw three snakes. The neighbours there say the more they kill. the thicker they seem to be."

Later the opportunity came to Mr. Winrod to make an observation of his own. While attending in a conference in Youngstown. he was taken by car to North Benton. He asked an old man if he could tell him where the Beddell grave was. "Sure. everybody around here knows where Chet Beddell was buried." said the old-timer. "You can't miss it—big monument in the graveyard. Looking for snakes?" Later. another man said. "Well. if Beddell did ask for snakes. he sure got 'em."

He and his companions came to the place in question where they saw the monument. the uplifted scroll. the other scroll under his foot. the stern bronze countenance. They approached the grave. camera in hand. Was it a hoax. or was it true? One of his companions was the first to see a snake. "Look there." he shouted. Yes! there it was. They walked round the grave and counted six snakes. His companion killed one. He photographed one. They also took other photographs. The sexton told them that he killed four that morning—he had killed as many as twenty snakes in a single day. Finally he said. "I don't know. maybe the Lord did have something to do with it."

—A. Naismith

34 Epigram

●I am an atheist. thank God!

—Anonymous

●Nobody talks so constantly about God as those who insist that there is no God.

—Heywood Brown

●To swear effectively men must make reference to God. Imagine. an atheistic evolutionist trying for a blood-curdling oath by swearing in the name of natural selection. or by the slimy. primeval amoeba.

—*Christianity Today*

●Calvin Coolidge once said: "It is hard to see how a great man can be an atheist. Doubters do not achieve. Skeptics do not contribute. Cynics do not create."

●G.K. Chesterton once said it is often supposed that when people stop believing in God. they believe in nothing. Alas. it is worse than that. When they stop believing in God. they believe in anything.

●Dostoevski remarked that "If God does not exist. everything is permissible."

●Napoleon said. "A man is not a man without God. I saw men without God in the reign of terror in 1793. One does not govern such men; he shoots them down.

●Atheism never composed a symphony. Never painted a masterpiece. Never dispelled a fear. Never healed a disease. Never gave peace of mind. Never dried a tear. Never established a philanthropy. Never gave an intelligent answer to the vast mystery of the universe. Never give meaning to man's life on earth. Never built a just and peaceful world. Never built a great and enduring civilization.

—Charles M. Houser

AUTOMOBILE

35 Never Forgave The Engine

In London England, lived Walter Lavender for eighty-five years. In all those eighty-five years, he never forgave the internal combustion engine for replacing the horse. He never rode in an automobile.

When he was dying, he stipulated a horse-drawn hearse. A film studio provided four bays and a splendid black carriage to carry him to his grave.

36 Those Antique Cars

About fifty years ago, the three prestige automobiles in the country were the Pierce Arrow, the Peerless, and the Packard. Then, the Hudson, Nash, and DeSoto—with the quarter of a billion dollar Edsel—have fallen by the wayside.

Of the 2,700 different domestic automobile name plates that have been registered in the US since 1893, fewer than two dozen remain. Time has passed the others by and buried them in the dust of competition.

37 US Highway System

The US has 3.8 million miles of highway, covering 33,000 square miles of land. The Interstate Highway System was started in 1956, about 90% of which has been completed. Total cost: $60 billion. It would cost another $30 billion, however, to complete the final 10%, due to inflation.

38 Fatal Days Of Week

According to insurance statistics, motor vehicle accident deaths are most frequent on Saturday, with Sunday running a close second. These two days together contribute approximately two-fifths of the accidents with fatal outcome. Holidays also are marked by a high toll of motor vehicle fatalities. Christmas Day, or one of the two days preceding it, usually is found to have the worst record for the year. New Year's Day also ranks high.

39 Hymns For Speeders

An Anglican clergyman has suggested suitable hymns for drivers who have the urge to speed:

At 75 miles an hour: "Nearer, My God, to Thee."

At 85 miles an hour: "When the Roll is Called Up Yonder, I'll Be there."

At 95 miles an hour: "Lord, I'm Coming Home."

—Christian Victory

25

B

BELIEF

40 I Believe

In a cellar in Cologne, Germany after World War II were found these words on the wall:

I BELIEVE ...
I believe in the sun,
    even when it is not shining;
I believe in love,
    even when I feel it not;
I believe in God,
    even when He is silent.

41 What Is Belief?

John G. Paton, pioneer missionary to the New Hebrides in the Pacific, was hard put to find a word for "believe," in the sense of trust, in the language of the South Sea Islanders, for whom he was translating the New Testament.

Finally he found the solution, by thus translating the answer of Paul and Silas to the question of the Philippian jailer, "What must I do to be saved?": "Lean your whole weight upon the Lord Jesus Christ and be saved."

42 Niagara Crowd's Mental Assent

A huge crowd was watching the famous tightrope walker, Blondin, cross Niagara Falls one day in 1860. He crossed it numerous times—a 1,000 foot trip, 160 feet above the raging waters. He asked the crowd if they believed he could take one person across. All assented. Then he approached one man and asked him to get on his back and go with him. The man refused! Mental assent or even verbal assent is not real belief.

BIBLE

43 Interesting Data

Books of Old Testament - 39.
Books of New Testament - 27.
Total number of books - 66.

Chapters in Old Testament - 929.
Chapters in New Testament - 260.
Total number chapters - 1,189.

Verses in Old Testament - 33,214.
Verses in New Testament - 7,959.
Total number of verses - 41,173.

Words in Old Testament - 593,393.
Words in New Testament - 181,253.
Total number of words - 774,746.

Letters in Old Testament - 2,738,100.
Letters in New Testament - 838,380.
Total number of letters - 3,566,480.
The shortest chapter is Psalm 117.
Ezra 7:21 contains all the letters of the alphabet except "j".
Esther 8:9 is the longest verse.
John 11:35 is the shortest verse.
There is no word of more than six syllables in the Bible.

44 Seven Wonders Of The Word

1. The wonder of its formation—the way in which it grew is one of the mysteries of time.

2. The wonder of its unification—a library of 66 books, yet one book.

3. The wonder of its age—most ancient of all books.

4. The wonder of its sale—best-seller of all time and of any other book.

5. The wonder of its interest—only book in the world read by all classes of people.

6. The wonder of its language—written largely by uneducated men, yet the best book from a literary standpoint.

7. The wonder of its preservation—the most hated of all books, yet it continues to exist.

—Speaker's Sourcebook

45 Franklin's Homemade Bible

That great American, Benjamin Franklin, loved to argue. Occasionally he would find himself overwhelmed by the arguments of his learned friends. At such times he often would say: "Give me a day to think the matter over, for I'm correct."

Meanwhile he would go to his print shop, set up some type in the style of the Bible, and express his position and argument in Bible language. He would then return next day to his opponents and proudly proclaim; "Whatever you may think, you cannot get away from the fact that Holy Scripture supports my argu-

ments. As it is said in the Book of John . . ." The ruse worked every time.

46 Statistics On Reading Time

It takes 70 hours and 40 minutes to read the Bible at pulpit rate.

It takes 52 hours and 20 minutes to read the Old Testament.

It takes the 18 hours and 20 minutes to read the New Testament.

In the Old Testament the Psalms take the longest to read: 4 hours and 28 minutes.

In the New Testament the Gospel of Luke takes 2 hours and 43 minutes to read.

—Eleanor Doan

47 Start Of Scofield Bible

One day in St. Louis, Missouri, a young convert named C.I. Scofield walked into the office of a friend. He found him with a new copy of the Scriptures on his desk and a pencil in his hand. "Why, man, you're spoiling that beautiful Bible!" exclaimed the young Christian.

His older friend pointed him to Acts 8, where he had underscored the fifth verse, "Then Philip went down to the city of Samaria, and preached Christ unto them." Then he had connected by a line to the eight verse which reads, "And there was great joy in that city.

Years afterward, Scofield frequently introduced his friend C.E. Paxson as "the man who first taught me to mark my Bible." The inspiration and instruction that Paxson gave him led to the preparation of the now-famous Scofield Reference Bible with its helpful footnotes and cross-references.

—Our Daily Bread

48 Standard Equipment On Pony Express

The pony express was a thrilling part of early American history. It ran from St.

Joseph, Missouri, to Sacramento, California—a distance of 1,900 miles. The trip was made in ten days. Forty men, each riding 50 miles a day, dashed along the trail on 500 of the best horses the West could provide.

To conserve weight, clothing was very light, saddles were extremely small and thin, and no weapons were carried. The horses themselves wore small shoes or none at all. The mail pouches were flat and very conservative in size. Letters had to be written on thin paper, and postage was $5.00 an ounce (a tremendous sum those days).

Yet, each rider carried a full-sized Bible! It was presented to him when he joined the pony express, and he took it with him despite all the scrupulous weight precautions.

—*Our Daily Bread*

49 Library Of Congress' Prettiest Book

The Library of Congress has millions of books. But its most beautiful volume is a Bible copied by a monk in the 16th century. Even the best printer in America or Europe cannot surpass its matchless perfection.

In this thousand-page Bible, are written in black ink the German text of the Scriptures. Each letter is perfect, without a scratch or blot anywhere. There are two columns to a page, and even under a magnifying glass, not the slightest irregularity of line space or letter formation can be noticed. At the beginning of each chapter, the first letter is very large—two to three inches long—and is brightly illuminated in red and blue ink. Then the figure of some saint or some incident narrated in the chapter is drawn into the inner spaces of the first letters.

Legend has it that a young man who had sinned deeply became a monk and determined to copy the Scriptures so that he might learn every letter of the Divine commands. For many years he pursued this self-imposed task, each letter wrought with reverence and love. When the last touch was given to the last letter, the old man (for he had became old) kissed the page and ended his work.

50 Oil From Sodom And Gomorrah

Some years ago Israeli businessman Xiel Federmann began to brood over the account of the destruction of Sodom and Gomorrah ("and, lo, the smoke of the country went up as the smoke of a furnace"), guessed that such conflagrations might indicate underground gas—and underground gas meant oil. He was right. In 1953 Israel's first oil well went into operation near the ancient site of Sodom and Gomorrah.

51 Epigram

●George Washington: "It is impossible to rightly govern the world without God and the Bible."

●John Quincy Adams: "So great is my veneration of the Bible, that the earlier my children begin to read it the more confident will be my hope that they will prove useful citizens of their country and respectable members of society."

●Charles Dickens: "The New Testament is the very best book that ever was or ever will be known in the world."

●Andrew Jackson: "That book, sir, is the rock on which our republic rests."

●Abraham Lincoln: "I believe the Bible is the best gift God has ever given to man. All the good from the Saviour of the world is communicated to us through this book."

●Horace Greeley: "It is impossible to mentally or socially enslave a Bible-reading people. The principles of the Bible are the groundwork of human freedom."

●Woodrow Wilson: "I ask every man and woman in this audience that from this day on they will realize that part of the destiny of America lies in their daily perusal of this great Book."

●Douglas MacArthur: "Believe me, sir, never a night goes by, be I ever so tired, but I read the Word of God before I go to bed."

●Herbert Hoover: "The whole of the inspirations of our civilization springs from the teachings of Christ and the lessons of the Prophets. To read the Bible for these fundamentals is a necessity of American life.

●Dwight D. Eisenhower: "To read the Bible is to take a trip to a fair land where the spirit is strengthened and faith renewed."

●Warning: This Book is habit-forming. Regular use causes loss of anxiety, decreased appetite for lying, cheating, stealing, hating. Symptoms: increased sensations of love, peace, joy, compassion.

52 Gideons In Action

A million copies every twenty-seven days. That, says the 47,000 member Gideons International, the rate at which its people are distributing Scriptures around the world. At the organization's seventy-sixth convention in Denver, leaders announced that 13.5 million Bibles and New Testaments had been distributed in 1975 in 107 countries and forty-three languages at a cost of $9.5 million.

Since 1908 nearly 150 million copies of Scripture have been distributed by the Gideons, a Protestant Christian business and professional men's association. A recent emphasis has been Scripture distribution among high school and college students. More than 600,000 New Testaments will be given to students in India, thanks to a single convention banquet offering.

—*Christianity Today*

53 Bible On The Moon

A microfilm packet containing Genesis 1:1 in sixteen languages and a complete RSV Bible were deposited on the moon by Apollo 14 LEM commander Edgar Mitchell.

BLOOD, THE

54 Atonement Verses In Bible

In the New Testament there are 290 references to the love of God, 290 times when God had declared His love for man. But in the same chapters and the same verses there are more than 1,300 references to the atonement, 1300 assurances that salvation can be had through the blood of Christ.

—G. Franklin Allee

55 House Of A Thousand Terrors

In the market place of Rotterdam, Holland, stood for many years an old corner house known as "The House of a Thousand Terrors." The story:

During the 16th century, the Dutch people rose in revolt against the cruel King Philip II of Spain. Philip sent a great army under the Duke of Alva to suppress the rebellion. Rotterdam held out for a time but finally capitulated.

From house to house the victors went, searching out citizens and then killing them in their houses. A group of men, women, and children were hiding in a corner house when they heard soldiers approaching. A thousand terrors griped their hearts. Then a young man had an idea. He took a goat in the house, killed it, and with a broom swept the blood under the doorway out to the street.

The soldiers reached the house and began to batter down the door. Noticing the blood coming out from under the door, one soldier said: "Come away, the work is already done here. Look at the blood beneath the door." And the people inside the house escaped.

56 "First Night Outside Paradise"

There is in Paris a famous picture by Zwiller called "The First Night Outside Paradise." Our first parents have been driven out of the Garden of Eden and are preparing to spend the first night in the desert beyond. In the distance can be discerned the figure of the angel with the flaming sword, but the eyes of the exiles are not fixed on him. They are gazing far above his head, and there, outlined in light—faint, but unmistakable—the artist has painted a cross. In wondering awe their gaze is fastened on it.

—Leslie Weatherhead

57 Rembrandt Crucified Christ

In the famous painting of the crucifixion by Rembrandt, your attention is drawn first to the dying Saviour. Then, as you notice the crowd gathered around that scene at Calvary, you are impressed by the various attitudes and actions of the people involved in putting the Son of God to death. Finally your eyes drift to the edge of the picture and catch sight of a lone figure almost hidden in the shadows. He represents the artist himself, for Rehbrandt realized that his sins had helped nail Jesus to the cross!

—Our Daily Bread

58 Man's Works In Heaven

"What work of man will there be in heaven?" Asks a minister one day. "None," replied the parishioner. "It will be the prints of the nails of the hands and feet of the Lord Jesus Christ." came the reply.

59 Amount Of Blood In Body

How many quarts of blood are there in the body? The amount of blood in the body varies from about 3½ to 5½ quarts or from 5 to 7 percent of body weight. It is possible to lose about one-third of this and still survive.

BOASTERS

60 No Women Sighted In Antarctic

Rear Adm. George J. Dufek, Naval commander of Operation Deepfreeze, tells this story of the day two airline stewardesses arrived on the only commercial plane ever to land in the antarctic:

"The girls, ravishing in furs, were being wined and dined in the McMurdo mess hall. But I noticed there were some men missing, and I walked around the base to see what they were doing. I found them sitting glumly in their quarters, smoking, drinking coffee and obviously resentful. Their reason? They wanted to be able to say that, from the time they left civilization until they returned, they hadn't seen a woman!"

—National Geographic

61 Perfection Personified

In basic training, our first sergeant made things very clear. He told us, "Don't question anything I say or tell you to do. Don't worry—I hardly ever make mistakes. Matter of fact, I've made only one mistake in my life. I once thought I was wrong about something. It turned out I wasn't."

—Dalex J. LeBlanc

62 Of Cows And Drums

Chang-three said, "We have a drum at home so big, when you beat it, it can be heard a hundred miles away."

Li-four said, "We have a cow in our home so big, when she takes a drink at the south bank of the river her head reaches out and touches the north bank."

Chang-three shook his head and exclaimed, "How could there be a cow of that size!"

Li-four said, "If there weren't cows of

this size, where would you get the hide to make that drum?"

　　　　　　　　　　　—Chinese Humor

63　Epigram

●We always weaken whatever we exaggerate.　—Jean Francois De Laharpe

●Few people need voice lessons to sing their own praise.　—E.C. Mckenzie

●The man who sings his own praises always gets the wrong pitch.

●Do you wish men to speak well of you? Then never speak well of yourself.
　　　　　　　　　　　　　　—Pascual

●If a fish escapes, it was a big one."
　　　　　　　　　　　—Malay Proverb

●Sign in front of an Atlanta restaurant featuring fried chicken: "If the Colonel Had Our Chicken Recipe He'd Be a General."　　　　　—Atlanta Journal

●James Michener confesses that he has been a jealous man ever since he heard of a Latin-American author who came up with a perfect book title: Complete Works, and Other Stories.
　　　　　　—New York Herald Tribune

●A huntsman, searching for a lion's tracks, asked a woodman if he had seen them and if he knew where its lair was. The man said he would show him the lion itself. At this the huntsman turned pale with fear and his teeth chattered. I am only looking for its trail, he said, not for the lion.

　　　　　　　　　　—Fables of Aesop

BOOKS

64　A Printed Book A Minute

The United States puts out 80,000 new books a year. The Soviet Union also issues 80,000 new books a year. Worldwide, over 500,000 new titles come off the presses in a single year—or about a new book a minute.

Total number of books printed around the world exceed eight billion a year. Most of these are circulated in the United States, Canada, New Zealand, Australia, and the Soviet Union.

65　All-Time Best-Sellers

The World Almanac and Book of Facts is the all-time best-selling book. Its cumulative sale has reached over 37,000,000 copies.

The Guinness Book of Records itself broke the record as the best-selling commercially-published book of all time. Its sales reached 24,000,000 copies in 1976. The previous record holder was Dr. Benjamin Spock's Common Sense Baby and Child Care.

The Guinness book was first brought out 20 years ago by a brewery company to resolve arguments in Britain's pubs. Its comprehensive coverage is well-known. Whatever superlatives one is interested in—the fastest, the earliest,the costliest, the nastiest—they are all listed here.

66　Books With 200-Year Guarantee

Late in 1973 a literary luncheon was held at the Savoy Hotel, London, England, to launch a limited edition of the complete collected works of Sir Winston Churchill. "The handsome 34-volume edition, bound in calfskin vellum and guaranteed to endure for at least 200 years, comprises 17,000 pages containing five million words by Churchill. Price tag on the set is $2,462."

67　Giant Libraries Around The World

According to the Guinness Book of Records, the largest library in the world is the Library of Congress in Washington, D.C. Founded in 1800, it accumulated over 74,000,000 items (including 16.5 million books) by 1973. The entire building has 35 acres of floor space and 327 miles of book shelves.

Another unique library is the Bibliotheque Nationale in Paris. It is one of the world's greatest libraries. It acquires everything published in France and tries to secure most French-language works printed around the world.

Still another is the Beutsche Bibliothek in Frankfurt, Germany. It arranges two million books on 19 kilometers of shelf space. It acquires at least one copy of every book published in West Germany and, if possible, gets a copy of everything written in German from all other countries.

68 The Nothing Book

When a New York publishing house brought out a volume of blank pages called *The Nothing Book*, it was accused of plagiarism by the Belgian publisher of a blank book called *The Memoirs of an Amnesiac*. The American firm rejected the claim, contending that blankness was in the public domain and therefore not subject to copyright restrictions.

— *United Press International*

69 He Was Killed By Typo

Baron de Grimm, in his *Memoirs*, mentioned a highly sensitive French author who died in a fit of anger. The reason: a favorite work of his was printed with over 300 errors, half of which were inserted by the proof-reader!

70 Famous People On Books

Cicero said that he would be willing to part with all he was worth so that he

might live and die among his books.

Petrarch was among books to the last, and was found dead with his books.

Leibnitz died with a book in his hand.

Buckle's last words: "My poor book!"

Scott shed tears when they wheeled him for the last time into his library.

Southey, towards his death sat up, stroked and kissed the books which he could no longer open or read.

— Cunningham Geikie

BOREDOM

71 Longest Continuous Yawn

The longest continuous yawning reported is by a 15 year-old female patient in 1888 who yawned continuously for 5 weeks.

72 The Doldrums

Nothing was so feared by seamen in the days when ocean vessels were driven by wind and sail as the doldrums. The doldrums is a part of the ocean near the equator, abounding calms, squalls, and light, baffling winds. There the weather is hot and extremely dispiriting. The old sailing vessels, when caught in doldrums, would lie helpless for days and weeks, waiting for the wind to begin to blow.

73 Doubling Away Boredom

During the late 19th century, the small towns of America had grown tired of seeing *Uncle Tom's Cabin* dramatized for over 40 years. To revive interest and instead of adopting a new play, the various Tom Companies just doubled the cast, having two Uncle Toms, two Little Evas, two Simon Legrees, and two sets of bloodhounds.

74 Joy Of Acquisition

The noted Count Henri-Francois-Noel of Paris owned a good-sized collection of rare books and loved that collection so much that he got bored with them. To stir up some excitement. he sold his entire library five times at five-year intervals (1837-1861) at auction.

He made certain he attended each auction and succeeded in outbidding all others. Thus—because of boredom—he sold and repurchased his entire library 5 times. The auctioneer's fee was 20% each time. and he ended up actually rebuying his own library after five auctions.

CHILDREN

75 Safest Age To Be

According to insurance statistics, age 10 is the safest year of life. Children of that age have passed the hazards of the acute infections of infancy and early childhood. They have yet to face the chronic diseases of the later years. Among children 10 years of age, however accidents constitute the most frequent cause of death.

76 First Few Years Crucial

How suggestive are the captions of recent magazine articles on children, written by leading educators, psychiatrists, and psychologists: "The First Five Years Shape All of Life"; "Behavior Is Set by Five"; "Baby's First Year Is the Growingest"; "Train Citizens in the Cradle"; "Don't Wait for the School Bell"; "Age Five Is Old Psychologically"; "Combat Crime in Infancy."

— *Walter B. Knight*

77 There's Hope For The Rest Of Us

Napoleon was number forty-two in his class. (Wonder who the forty one were ahead of him?)

Sir Isaac Newton was next to the lowest in his class. He failed in geometry because he didn't do his problems according to the book.

George Eliot learned to read with great difficulty, giving no promise of brilliance in her youth.

James Russell Lowell was suspended from Harvard for complete indolence.

Oliver Goldsmith was at the bottom of his class.

James Watt was the butt of jokes by his schoolmates.

— *Speaker's Sourcebook*

78 They Were Saved In Childhood

Polycarp, the courageous early church martyr, was converted at 9 years old. Jonathan Edwards, perhaps the mightiest intellect of the American pulpit, was saved at 7. Count Zinzendorf, leader of the Moravians, signed his name to this covenant when he was 4: "Dear Saviour, do Thou be mine and I will be Thine!"

Matthew Henry, that great commentator, was converted at 11. Robert Hall, the prince of Baptist preachers, received Christ at 12. Spurgeon began to awaken spiritually at 12. Isabella Graham, immortal in the Christian Church, was converted at 10.

79 Wesley's Mother On Child Raising

John and Charles Wesley, were reared by a God-fearing mother (of seventeen) who laid down some excellent principles for child training. They appear in John Wesley's Journal:

"When turned a year old (and some before), they were taught to fear the rod, and to cry softly; by which means they escaped abundance of correction they might otherwise have had; and that most odious noise of the crying of children was rarely heard in the house; but the family usually lived in as much quietness as if there had not been a child among them.

"In order to form the minds of children, the first thing to be done is to conquer the will, and bring them to an obedient temper. To inform the understanding is a work of time, and must with children proceed by slow degrees as they are able to bear it: but subjecting the will is a thing which must be done at once; and the sooner the better. For by neglecting timely correction they will contract a stubbornness and obstinacy which is hardly ever after conquered.

"Whenever a child is corrected, it must be conquered; and this will be no hard matter to do, if it be not grown headstrong by too much indulgence ... I cannot yet dismiss this subject. Self-will is the root of all sin and misery, so whatever cherishes this in children insures their after-wretchedness; whatever checks and mortifies it promotes their future happiness."

CHRIST-CENTEREDNESS

80 Century-Old Prayer

There is a fifteen-hundred-year-old prayer which still stirs our hearts. It is particularly inspiring and helpful to those who want to follow Christ. It is called "St. Patrick's Breastplate."

Here is part of it: Christ be with me, Christ in the front, Christ in the rear, Christ within me, Christ below me, Christ above me, Christ at my right hand, Christ at my left, Christ in the fort, Christ in the Chariot seat, Christ at the helm, Christ in the heart of every man who thinks of me, Christ in the mouth of every man who speaks to me, Christ in every eye that sees me, Christ in every ear that hears me.

81 Dr. Gordon's Dream

Dr. A.J. Gordon, while preparing his Sunday sermon, was so tired that he fell asleep in his study. He dreamed that it was the next morning in the pulpit and the church was packed. A stranger walked in and a deacon let him have his seat. The stranger was so commanding yet attentive, and Gordon found himself as if speaking to him alone. He decided to meet this stranger after church.

As the congregation filed out one by one, the pastor (in his dream) looked in vain for the stranger until everyone was home. "Do you know him?" he asked the deacon. "Why, yes. He is Jesus Christ." "Oh, how I wished I could have talked with him!" Gordon lamented. "It is alright, pastor," assured the deacon, "He'll be back next Sunday."

Gordon awoke, realizing in a new way that everytime he preaches and speaks about Jesus, Christ is in the midst and hears every word. This dream revived both pastor and church. Gordon preached with a new power. He established "Salvation Centers" in Boston, gave great sums to missions, to weak churches, to the

Jews, to the Chinese. He started a school to train missionaries. He died at age 59 with "Victory" on his lips.

82 Leonardo De Vinci's Cup

When Leonardo de Vinci was forty-three years old, the Duke Ludovinco of Milan asked him to paint the dramatic scene of Jesus' last supper with his disciples.

Working slowly and giving meticulous care to details, he spent three years on the assignment. He grouped the disciples into threes, two groups on either side of the central figure of Christ. Christ's arms are outstreched. In his right hand, He holds a cup, painted beautifully with marvelous realism.

When the masterpiece was finished, the artist said to a friend, "Observed it and give me your opinion of it!"

"It's wonderful!" exclaimed the friend. "The cup is so real I cannot divert my eyes from it!"

Immediately Leonardo took a brush and drew it across the sparkling cup! He exclaimed as he did so: "Nothing shall detract from the figure of Christ!"

83 Patriotism Not Enough

Edith Cavell, the British nurse killed by Germans in World War I, was captured. Just before the bandage was placed over her eyes for the firing squad, she said: "I am glad to die for my country. But I realize that patriotism is not enough." Then she gave clear and definite testimony to her personal faith in the Lord Jesus Christ, and assurance of salvation. She died under the firing squad in 1915.

84 Old John Jasper's First
   ## Desire In Heaven

Old John Jasper, that former slave after the War between the States pastored the Sixth Mt. Zion Baptist Church in Richmond, Virginia. Somebody asked him if there had been five preceding Mt. Zion Baptist Churches and that was why they called it the "Sixth." He said, "No, we just liked the name."

Old John Jasper pastored a great church. He was speaking to his congregation one day on heaven and the joys which will await us on the other side. He tried to describe those beauties, the joys ineffable and full of glory. His vivid imagination and his emotions were caught up and as he opened his mouth to speak he couldn't say a word. He tried several times and the great crowd sat there in anticipatory silence. He tried again but still no sound.

Then they saw the tears roll down his black cheeks. Still as he would try to articulate, not a sound could he make. Finally, he shook his head and waved his crowd toward the exit, but that great audience just sat there as if enthralled. After several attempts to no avail, he walked back to the side of the pulpit and had his hand upon the door which led to his study, and again he waved the crowd toward the exit but they still wait there.

Seeing that they wouldn't leave, he composed himself and walked back toward the edge of the pulpit and leaning over it said something like this, "Brothers and sisters, when I think of the glory which shall be revealed in us, I can visualize that day when old John Jasper's last battle has been fought and the last burden has been borne. I can visualize that day when this tired servant of God shall lay down his burdens and walk up to the battlements of the City of God. Then as I stand outside the beautiful gate, I can almost hear the Mighty Angel on guard say, "John Jasper, you want your shoes?"

"I'se gonnay say, 'Course I wants ma shoes, ma golden slippers to walk the gold-paved streets of the City of God, but not now.'

"Then I can hear the Mighty Angel as

he says, 'John Jasper, don't you want your robe?'

"I'se gonnay say, 'Course I wants ma robe, that robe of linen clean and white which am the righteousness of the saints, but not now.'

"Then the Angel would say, 'John Jasper, you want your crown?

"I shall say, 'Course, Mighty Angel, I wants all the reward that's comin' to me, this poor black servant of the Lamb, but not now.'

Then the Angel would say, 'John Jasper, wouldn't you like to see Elijah, the great prophet, who called down fire from heaven, wouldn't you like to shake hands with John the beloved disciple who leaned on the Master's breast at the Last Supper? Wouldn't you like to shake hands with Paul, the great apostle to the Gentiles, the greatest church establisher and soul-winner of all time?

"I'll say, 'Course, Mighty Angel. I wants to know and to shake hands and to commune with those, the saints of God who have won the incorruptible crown. Yes, I have some loved ones over here I wants to see, too, but not now. Fust, I wants to see Massa Jesus .... I wants to see Him fust of all.'"

—G. Beauchamp Vick

CHURCH ATTENDANCE

85 U.S. Church Attendance Statistics

Church and synagogue attendance in the United States rose in 1976—the first time that has happened since 1958, according to a Gallup Poll.

The poll interviewed 13,398 persons over age 17 in more than 300 localities during nine selected weeks. Forty-two percent said they had attended church or synagogue during the preceding seven days, an increase of 2 percent over the past five years. A high of 49 per cent was recorded in 1955 and 1958, said Gallup.

The study shows that 55 per cent of Roman Catholics are in church in a typical week, 40 per cent of Protestants. Women still make up a majority of those in the pews: 46 per cent of the nation's women attend, 37 per cent of the men.

Least likely attenders are people living in the West and people under age 30; those in the South and Middle West have the best attendance record.

—Christianity Today

86 Church Good For Your Health

A John Hopkins University medical researcher has just discovered what the Presbyterian Ministers' Life Insurance Fund has known for more than two centuries: attending church is good for your health.

The risk of fatal heart diseases is almost twice as high for the non-churchgoer than for men who attend once a week or more, according to a study made by Dr. George W. Comstock of the university's Department of Epidemiology. The doctor also observed that the "clean life" associated with regular churchgoing appears to be statistically related to a lower incidence of other major diseases, adding that going to church is a very favorable input.

—Selected

87 Attending Church 88 Years

"Aunt Effie" Linquist has attended the First Baptist Church in Keokuk, Iowa, regularly for the last 88 years. Since 1888, she hasn't missed a Christmas or Easter service. During that time 15 different pastors have served her church. She has listened to over 8,000 sermons, attended more than 4,000 prayer meetings, and said over 29,000 bedtime prayers.

Mrs. Linquist taught Sunday school for over 50 years, and several of her former Sunday school students are now in the ministry.

—Have a Good Day

88 The Perfect Church

I think that I shall never see
A Church that's all it ought to be:
A Church whose members never stray
Beyond the Strait and Narrow Way;
A Church that has no empty pews,
Whose Pastor never has the blues,
A Church whose Deacons always deak,
And none is proud, and all are meek;
Where gossips never peddle lies,
Or make complaints or criticize;
Where all are always sweet and kind,
And all to other's faults are blind.
Such perfect Churches there may be,
But none of them are known to me.
But still, we'll work, and pray and plan,
To make our own the best we can.

—Selected

89 Possible To Be Christian Without Church?

Question: Can I be a Christian without joining the church?

Answer: Yes, it is possible. It is something like being:

A student who will not go to school.
A soldier who will not join an army.
A citizen who does not pay taxes or vote.
A salesman with no customers.
An explorer with no base camp.
A seaman on a ship without a crew.
A businessman on a deserted island.
An author without readers.
A tuba player without an orchestra.
A parent without a family.
A football player without a team.
A politician who is a hermit.
A scientist who does not share his findings.
A bee without a hive.

—Wesleyan Christian Advocate

90 "Praise Him ... Here We Go!"

A little five-year-old girl had been attending the church kindergarten. Each day before the children were dismissed, the teacher had them sing the Doxology, which the little five-year-old loved to sing, but in her own words: "Praise God from whom all blessings flow, Praise Him all creatures, here we go!"

—Christian Parent

91 Epigram

●"Everybody has a reason for staying home from church—even those who are here"

●Some people think a 30-minute sermon is too long, so they substitute a 300-column Sunday paper.

●The reason why people miss church when it rains is the reason why we have church.

●Wanted: Men, women and children to sit in slightly used pews Sunday morning—Saratoga Congregational Church.

—In "Wanted" section of
St. Charles, Minnesota Press

●If absence makes the heart grow fonder, some people ought to love their church greatly.

●A certain congregation had dwindled in size so much that when the minister said "Dearly Beloved," the maiden lady in the front row thought he was proposing.

—Speaker's Sourcebook

●The church is not a club of saints, it is a hospital for sinners.

●A man proudly said: "I go to church only 2 times in my life—the first time they sprinkle water on me the second time they sprinkle rice."

A hearer added: "And the third time, they sprinkle dirt."

●"Most people think of the church as a drama, with the minister as the chief actor, God as the prompter, and the laity as the critic. What is actually the case is that the congregation is the chief actor, the minister is the prompter, and God is the critic."

—James Kennedy

CIGARETTES

92 American Smoking Statistics

Americans are the heaviest smokers in the world, burning up an average of 4,300 cigarettes per adult per year. The 607,000 million cigarettes thus consumed in 1975 cost smokers $13,000,000,000.

93 Reducing Your Years

The former president of the American College of Surgeons, Dr. Alton Ochsner, said: "Of the 30,000 men and women who will die of lung cancer the next year, death in 95th of the cases will be traceable to smoking. Each cigarette costs the smoker 14.4 minutes of his life.

Dr. Linus Pauling, two-time Nobel prize-winning chemist, told the students of the University of Toronto: "If everyone were to stop smoking, the overall life expectancy would rise by four years."

This is based on the fact that a person who smokes a pack a day from twenty years of age on has his life expectancy reduced by eight years. Studies also reveal that a 50-year-old person who has never smoke will live an average eight and a half years longer than a person who smokes a pack a day, and seventeen years longer than one who smokes two packs a day.

94 How To Shrink Dogs

"When I was in Paris some years ago," said a noted lecturer, "I met a man who had very tiny dogs for sale. I asked him why they were so abnormally small.

"At first he refused to tell me, fearing that I would divulge his secret or become his business competitor. I convinced him that I was simply in pursuit of knowledge. Then, with many cautions, he confided to me his process for producing these very tiny dwarfs.

" 'You see, I put a little speck of *nicotine* in their food when they are quite

young. Then I add a little more, and a little more, and then they never get big.' "

"But doesn't the nicotine ever kill them?"

" 'Oh, yes many of them die; but I get a big price for the little fellows that live.' "

Poor dogs, thus poisoned for the sake of gain.

—White Ribbon

95 Postponing The Temptation

An Army doctor in Texas has suggested a method for losing the tobacco habit which milht work for some people. Each day the smoker postpones for one hour longer that first cigarette.

On the first day, as many cigarettes as desired may be smoked. On the second day, the first cigarette is put off for one hour, but after that the smoker consumes as many as he wishes. On the third day, no cigarettes are smoked until two hours after rising, but, again, as many thereafter as are craved. If the program is carried out, smoking will cease in about two weeks. The theory is that, if the smoker can consume an unlimited number of cigarettes after his period of abstinence, he loses his fear of the program.

—Ladies' Home Journal

CONSCIENCE

96 On With The Card Game

Madame du Deffant was noted in the high society of France as a bel-esprit before the period of the first French Revolution. Death seized her whilst in the act of playing at cards, in the midst of a circle of her frivolous and thoughtless friends. So little concerned was the rest of the party at the solemn event which had just occurred, that they resolved, with a hardened indifference rarely to be equalled, to play out their game before they gave the alarm.

—Walter Baxendale

97 Government's Conscience Fund

In a special office of the Treasury Department is located the government's Conscience Fund. It represents a unique service for those who have cheated on Uncle Sam. The Fund is now $3 million after 160 years.

It all started back in 1811 when a New York man sent in $6 who said he was "suffering the most painful pangs of conscience." The biggest year of conscience settlement—no one knows the reason— was 1950 when $370,285 came in. The largest contribution was $14,250 from London in the late nineteenth century.

Along with the money came notes of explanations and appeals for forgiveness. "I'll sleep better now," wrote a donor. "I have my suitcase packed for heaven," another confided. "I want to have a clear conscience," still another. And "I'd hate to burn in hell for a couple of bucks."

98 "He Is Alive To Me"

A follower of Pythagoras once bought a pair of shoes from a cobbler, promising to pay him on a future day. That day came, and he took the money. But finding the cobbler passed away, he secretly rejoiced that he could retain the money and get a pair of shoes for nothing. But his conscience would allow him no rest. And taking the money, he went back to the cobbler's shop, cast in the money, and said: "Go thy way; for, though he is dead to all the world, yet he is alive to me."

—Foster

99 "Fly At Once, All Discovered"

It is said that Sir Arthur Conan Doyle, the master writer of mystery stories, had a very feeble sense of humor. Nevertheless, in one of his fiendish tales he introduced a joke with grim humor. He chose a dozen friends and to each one sent the same telegram with the same words: "Fly at once; all is discovered."

Within 24 hours not one of the twelve remained in the country.

—Arthur Tonne

CONSECRATION

100 Livingstone's Last Birthday

When Stanley found Livingstone, the great missionary who spent thirty years in darkest Africa, he wanted him to come back to England with him, but Livingstone refused to go. Two days later he wrote in his diary: "March 19, my birthday. My Jesus, my King, my Life, my all, I again dedicate my whole self to Thee. Accept me, and grant, O gracious Father, that ere the year is gone I may finish my work. In Jesus' name I ask it. Amen." A year later his servants found him on his knees dead.

—Tom M. Olson

101 Florence Nightingle At 30

Florence Nightingale at thirty wrote in her diary, "I am thirty years of age, the age at which Christ began His mission. Now no more childish things, no more vain things. Now, Lord, let me think only of Thy will." Years later, near the end of her illustrious, heroic life she was asked for her life's secret, and she replied, "Well, I can only give one explanation. That is, I have kept nothing back from God."

—Paul Rees

102 A Swiss Hermit

Pleaded Nicholas of Flue, Swiss holy hermit, "O Lord, take from me what keeps me from Thee; give me what brings me to Thee; and take myself and give me Thyself!"

103 Jim Elliot's Diary

In a diary entry, Jim Elliot, the Auca Indian martyr, wrote, "God, I pray Thee,

light these idle sticks of my life, that I
may burn for Thee. Consume my life, my
God, for it is Thine. I seek not a long life,
but a full one, like You, Lord Jesus."
— *The Bible Friend*

104 I See Myself
One day I looked at myself,
At the self that Christ can see;
I saw the person I am today
And the one I ought to be.

I saw how little I really pray,
How little I really do;
I saw the influence of my life-
How little of it was true!

I saw the bundle of faults and fears
I ought to lay on the shelf;
I had given a little bit to God,
But I hadn't given myself.

I came from seeing myself,
With the mind made up to be
The sort of person that Christ can use
With a heart He may always see.
— *Selected*

CONVERSIONS

105 Change On Pitcairn Island
The true story of the *Mutiny on the
Bounty* has often been retold. One part
that deserves retelling was the transfor-
mation wrought by one book. Nine
mutineers with six native men and twelve
native (Tahitian) women put ashore on
Pitcairn Island in 1790. One sailor soon
began distilling alcohol, and the little colony was plunged into debauchery and
vice.

Ten years later, only one white man
survived, surrounded by native women
and half-breed children. In an old chest
from the *Bounty*, this sailor one day found
a Bible. He began to read it and then to
teach it to the others. The result was that
his own life and ultimately the lives of all
those in the colony were changed. Dis-

covered in 1808 by the *USS Topas*, Pitcairn had become a prosperous community with no jail, no whisky, no crime,
and no laziness.
— *Gospel Herald*

106 Sequel To Crusoe
Few persons, I suppose, have read the
sequel to Robinson Crusoe's story of his
captivity on the lonely island in which
Crusoe tells how he revisited the island
and endeavored to convert to Christianity
the mixed colony of English and natives.

Most notorious among these islanders
was the wicked and profligate seaman
Will Atkins. After his conscience had
been reached and it was suggested to
Atkins that he and his companions teach
their wives religion, he responded, "Lord,
sir, how should we teach them religion?
Should we talk to them of God and Jesus
Christ, and heaven and hell, it would
make them laugh at us.

In his ever charming style Defoe
describes Atkins sitting by the side of his
tawny wife under the shade of a bush and
trying to tell her about God, occasionally
going off a little distance to fall on his
knees to pray, until at length they both
knelt down together, while the friend
who was watching with Crusoe cried out,
"St. Paul! St Paul behold he prayeth."
— *C. E. Macarthey*

107 Origin Of "Ben Hur"
Two infidels once sat on a railroad
train, discussing the life of Christ. One of
them said, "I think an interesting romance
could be written about him." The other
replied, "And you are just the man to
write it. Tear down the prevailing sentiment about His divinity, and paint Him as
a man—a man among men."

The suggestion was acted upon and the
romance written. The man who made the
suggestion was Colonel Ingersoll, the
noted atheist. The writer was General

Lew Wallace, and the book was called *Ben Hur*.

In the process of constructing the life of Christ, Gen. Wallace found himself facing the greatest life ever lived on earth. The more he studied, the more he was convinced Christ was more than man. Until one day, he was forced to cry "Verily, this was the Son of God!"

108 Story Of John D. Rockefeller

John D. Rockefeller, Sr. was strong and husky when small. He early determined to earn money and drove himself to the limit. At age 33, he earned his first million dollars. At age 43, he controlled the biggest company in the world. At age 53, he was the richest man on earth and the world's only billionaire.

Then he developed a sickness called "alopecia," where the hair of his head dropped off, his eyelashes and eyebrows disappeared, and he was shrunken like a mummy. His weekly income was one million dollars, but he digested only milk and crackers. He was so hated in Pennsylvania that he had to have body-guards day and night. He could not sleep, stopped smiling long since, and enjoyed nothing in life.

The doctors predicted he would not live over one year. The newspaper had gleefully written his obituary in advance—for convenience in sudden use. Those sleepless nights set him thinking. He realized with a new light that he "could not take one dime into the next world." Money was not everything.

The next morning found him a new man. He began to help churches with his amassed wealth; the poor and needy were not overlooked. He established the Rockefeller Foundation whose funding of medical researches led to the discovery of penicillin and other wonder drugs. John D. began to sleep well, eat and enjoy life.

The doctors had predicted he would not live over age 54. He lived up to 98.

109 Col. Sanders Found The Secret

In his autobiography, Col. Harland Sanders of Kentucky Fried Chicken fame says that he was always a God-fearing man. In every venture he gave God a tenth of the profits. Yet he knew that if he died, God probably wouldn't take him to heaven.

Woried, he traveled to Australia to a special church convention for the answer. He didn't find it.

One day, Sanders was walking down a street in Louisville, Kentucky, when there Rev. Waymon Rodgers of Louisville's Evangel Tabernacle invited him to some evangelistic services. Several days later, Sanders went. At age 79, he claimed the promises of Rom. 10:9. "When I walked out of that church that night, I knew I was a different man. All my tithing and good deeds had never given me the sense of God's presence that I knew then," he says.

110 Ty Cobb's Deathbed Conversion

Then there is Ty Cobb, that all-time great who played 3,033 games and for 12 years led the American League in batting average. For four years, he batted over 400. On his death bed, July 17, 1961, he accepted Jesus Christ as his Saviour. He said, "You tell the boys I'm sorry it was the last part of the ninth that I came to know Christ. I wish it had taken place in the first half of the first."

COURAGE

111 Hated But Happy Young Girl

Ye shall be hated of all men for my name's sake (Matt. 10:22). The Russian newspaper published by the Young Communist League once printed a letter from Nina K., a sixteen-year-old girl, quoting her as saying, "I am a young Communist League member. I am a normal girl, but at the same time I am unusual. I'm a Baptist! Frankly, I do not consider myself a mem-

ber of the Young Communist League. I have Komsomol members pass me without greeting. Let them look upon with contempt. My brothers and sisters in God treat me very well. I believe them and I believe God." The paper captioned the letter "The One Who Has Gone Astray."
                                              —Tom M. Olson

112 Pastor Says: "Shoot Away"
During the pastorate of Henry Ward Beecher in Indianapolis he preached a series of sermons upon drunkenness and gambling, incidentally scoring the men of the community who profited by these sins. During the ensuing week he was accosted on the street by a would-be assailant, pistol in hand, who demanded a retraction of some utterance of the preceding Sunday.

"Take it back, right here!" he demanded with an oath, or "I will shoot you on the spot!"

"Shoot away!" was the preacher's response as he walked calmly away, hurling over his shoulder this parting remark:

"I don't believe you can hit the mark as well as I did!"
                                              —Gospel Herald

113 Only One Thing Pained Chrysostom
When the great Chrysostom was arrested by the Roman Emperor, the latter sought to make the Greek Christian recant, but without success. So the emperor discussed with his advisers what could be done to the prisoner. "Shall I put him in a dungeon?" the Emperor asked.

"No," one of his counsellors replied, "for he will be glad to go. He longs for the quietness wherein he can delight in the mercies of his God."

"Then he shall be executed!" said the Emperor.

"No," was the answer, "for he will also be glad to die. He declares that in the event of death he will be in the presence of his Lord."

"What shall we do then?" the ruler asked.

There is only one thing that will give Chrysostom pain," the counsellor said. "To cause Chrysostom to suffer, make him sin. He is afraid of nothing except sin."
                                              —Baptist Standard

114 Wanted: Hundred Men
John Wesley said, "Give me a hundred men who fear nothing but sin, and desire nothing but God, and I will shake the world: I care not a straw whether they be clergymen or laymen; and such alone will overthrow the kingdom of Satan and build up the Kingdom of God on earth."
                                              —The Preacher's Magazine

115 Epigram
●Courage is not the absence of fear; it is the mastery of it.

●Said William Penn: "Right is right, even if everyone is against it, and wrong is wrong, even if everyone is for it."

●Oh, do not pray for easy lives. Pray to be stronger men. Do not pray for task equal to your powers. Pray for powers equal to your tasks.

COURTSHIP

116 Legal Value Of Kiss: $275,000
DETROIT, Michigan (UPI)—Clare Tomie told a Wayne county circuit court jury she doesn't feel a thing when she kisses her husband, and the jury decided the lack of sensation was worth $275,000.

Mrs. Tomie, who was awarded $260,000 said a dental operation left her lower lip and lower jaw permanently numb and had caused a strain in her relationship with her husband.

The jury of four women and two men also awarded her husband $15,000.

In the operation, Mrs. Tomie said, a part of a drill broke and imbedded in her jaw. Later, an X-ray disclosed a bit of metal in her jaw. It was removed, she said, but the numbness remained.

The couple sued a Detroit oral surgeons group, which said it would seek a new trial.

117 For A Year—A Dead Duck!

A Wisconsin clergyman usually has a premarriage conference with couples planning a wedding, and one of the questions he asks is how long they have known each other.

"Nine times out of ten," says the minister, "the groom will answer, 'Two or three years,' while the bride will say, 'Three or four years.' In other words, she has had her eye on him, and he has been a dead duck for a year before he knew anything about it."

—Milwaukee *Journal*

118 He Waited 48 Years

This time Madge Coomber's 89-year-old father gave his permission, and so Madge and Len Patching were married— 48 years after Len was first rejected and went off to live in Australia.

"Madge was the only girl I ever loved," said the groom. "I never married. I always knew that one day I would come back and find her."

Last summer after retiring as a technical college instructor in New South Wales, he flew back to Britain to search for the woman he last knew as a childhood sweetheart of 17.

He located her, now a widow, with the help of a local radio station. Within weeks they were engaged.

119 Solomon As Better Judge

When William Jennings Bryan went to call on the father of his prospective wife and seek the hand of his daughter in marriage, knowing the strong religious feeling of the father, he thought to strengthen his case by a quotation from the Bible, and quoted the proverb of Solomon: "Whoso findeth a wife findeth a good thing" (Prov. 18:22).

But to his surprise the father replied with a citation from Paul to the effect that he that marrieth doeth well, but he that marrieth not doeth better. The young suitor was for a moment confounded. Then with a happy inspiration he replied that Paul had no wife and Solomon had seven hundred, and Solomon, therefore, ought to be the better judge as to marriage.

—C. E. Macartney

120 Epigram

●Puppy love has sent many a young man to the dogs.

●To marry a woman for her beauty is like buying a house for its paint.

●The greatest salesman in the world is not a man—it's a girl selling her boy friend the engagement ring!

—Maxwell Droke

●The teen-ager sent his girl friend her first orchid with this note: "With all my love and most of my allowance."

●"To lovers, even pockmarks look like dimples."   —Japanese

●Heard during a news report on the radio: "Efforts are being made to avert a threatened strike of stewardesses and pursuers."

●A draftee claimed exemption on the grounds of poor eyesight—and brought his wife along to prove it.

—*The Ohio Motorist*

●In the bakery department of a Dallas supermarket, a wedding cake was set out for shoppers with the sign: "He changed his mind. Have a piece of cake on us."

—*Forth Worth Star-Telegram*

COVETOUS

121 Needs Another Hundred Thousand

The first assignment I give to my classes in Basic English is a composition on "What I Would Do If I Had a Million Dollars." My students are a delightful potpourri of Americans of all ages and colors, including immigrants from five continents, and young foreign students.

The latest class was pin-drop quiet for 30 minutes, while the students struggled to express their dreams in English. Then a ponderously built senora stalked up to my desk and flung down two pages of crossed-out and written-over figures.

"Not enough, teacher!" she proclaimed in disgust. "I gotta have another hundred thousand!"

—*Reader's Digest*

122 Could Be Spot Of Hell

Scott Fitzgerald, famous novelist of our day, had just died and on his desk was found a plot for a new novel. He was going to write a book in which a wealthy man died and left a strange will. The will bequeathed all of his millions to be divided equally, share and share alike, to all his relatives. There was one condition. They were to come and live together in his spacious mansion. Below the outlined plot was a note. "This could be a little spot of hell."

123 Man's Only Real Right

In Tolstoy's *Man and Dame*, Fortune the hero is told he can have the right to all of the land around which he can plow a furrow in a single day. The man started off with great vigor, and was going to encompass only that which he could easily cared for. But as the day progressed he desired more and more rights. He plowed and plowed, until at the end of the day he could in no possible way return to his original point of departure, but struggling to do so, he fell, the victim of a heart attack. The only right he secured was the right to 18 square feet of land in which he was buried.

124 "Let Her Be Generous"

A small boy was given two apples and told to divide them with his sister, and in doing so to be generous in giving her the larger one. He said finally, "Look Ma, you give her the apples and ask her to be generous."

125 "He Wants You!"

A doctor, who had doctored a man's son to death and was threatened with legal proceedings, agreed to hand over his own son for adoption. Later on, he managed to cause the death of a client's servant, and was obliged to give up the only servant he had. One night there came a knock at his door from a neighbor, who said: "My wife is having a baby. Please come and attend to her at once!"

"Ah, the blackguard!" cried the doctor to his wife. "I know what he wants this time—he wants you."

—*Chinese Humor*

CRITICISMS

126 Criticizing Causes Nervousness

David H. Fink, author of *Release From Nervous Tension*, wrote an article for the *Coronet Magazine*, in which he made a striking suggestion as to how we can overcome mental and emotional tensions.

As a psychiatrist for the Veterans' Administration he was familiar with 10,000 case histories in this field. Thousands of people, who were mentally and emotionally "tied up" had asked Dr. Fink for some short, magic-button cure for nervousness. In his search for such a cure he studied two groups: the first group was made up of thousands of people who were suffering from mental and emotional disturbances: the second group contained only those. thousands of them. who were free from such tensions.

Gradually one fact began to stand out: those who suffered from extreme tension had one trait in common—they were habitual faultfinders. constant critics of people and things around them. Whereas the men and women who were free of all tensions were the least faultfinding. It would seem that the habit of criticizing is a prelude or mark of the nervous. and of the mentally unbalanced.

127 Customers Will Run It

What Simeon Ford, the proprietor of the Old Grand Union Hotel in New York. had to say about hotels in particular might readily apply to almost any business.

"You don't need to know anything about a hotel to run one," he said. "You just open up and the customers tell you how to run it."

128 The Wrecking Crew

I stood on the streets of a busy town.
Watching men tearing a building down:
With a "Ho. heave. ho." and a lusty yell.
They swung a beam and a sidewall fell.

I asked the foreman of the crew.
"Are those men as skilled as those you'd
   hire if you wanted to build?"
"Ah. no." he said. "no indeed.
Just common labor is all I need.

I can tear down as much in a day or two.
As would take skilled men a year to do."
And then I thought as I went on my way.
Just which of these two roles am I trying
   to play?

Have I walked life's road with care.
Measuring each deed with rule and
   square?
Or am I one of those who roam the town.
Content with the labor of tearing down?
                              —Selected

129 In Heaven

Hans Priem was admitted into paradise on condition that he was not to indulge in his habit of criticising and censuring whatever he notice. He saw two angels carrying a beam crossways, and knocking it against every object they met; but he said nothing. He next saw two other angels drawing water from a fountain and pouring it into a barrel which had holes in the bottom; but he held his peace. Many things similarly were noticed, but he suppressed his remarks, fearing that he might otherwise be expelled from the place.

At last. he saw a cart stuck in the mud. with one pair of horses yoked into its front. and another pair yoked to its rear—the driver urging both simultaneously forward. This was more than Hans could take. and he started criticising, when he was seized by two angels and turned to the door.

Before the door closed behind him. he looked back and saw that the horses were *winged* horses. and were pulling the cart from the mud into the air; and as for the cases of the beam and the barrel, there were equally good reasons for what was one.

                              —Gotthold

130 I Do The Best I Know

Abraham Lincoln once said, "If I tried to read. much less answer, all the criticisms made of me. and all the attacks leveled against me. this office would have to be closed for all other business. I do the best I know how, the very best I can. And I mean to keep on doing this. down to the very end. If the end brings me out all wrong, ten angels swearing I had been right would make no difference. If the end brings me out all right, then what is said against me now will not amount to anything."

131 Epigram

●Pay no attention to what the critics say; there has never been set up a state in honor of a critic.   —Jean Sibelius

●When you make your mark in the world, watch out for guys with erasers.
          —*The Wall Street Journal*

●"If a dog barks at a hill, will the hill crumble?"   —Malay Proverbs

●If criticism had any real power to harm, the skunk would be extinct by now.
          —Fred Allen

●The moon could not go on shining if it paid any attention to the little dogs that bark at it.

●If you are standing upright, don't worry if your shadow is crooked.

●Be not disturbed at being misunderstood; be disturbed rather at not being understanding.   —Chinese Proverb

●"I want to be willing to make enemies because of my position but not because of my disposition." —Jack Hyles

●Criticism may not be agreeable, but it is necessary. It fulfills the same function as pain in the human body: it calls attention to an unhealthy state of things.
          —*Reader's Digest*

●The trouble with most of us is that we would rather be ruined by praise than saved by criticism.
          —Norman Vincent Peale

●The only gracious way to accept an insult is to ignore it, stop it; if you can't stop it, laugh at it; if you can't laugh at it, it's probably deserved.
          —Russell Lynes

D

DEATHS

132 Total Deaths In World
The number of deaths in the world may fluctuate widely from one year to the next. A rough estimate of annual deaths is 60,000,000 or about 2 every second.

About two-thirds of these deaths are in Asia, a little less than one-sixth in Europe, about one-tenth in Africa, and one-twelfth in the Western Hemisphere.

In comparison, there are about 3 births every second, as there are between 100 and 115 million babies every year. About three-fifths of the births are in Asia, one-eight each in Europe and in the Americas, and one-tenth in Africa.

133 Person's Death Ages
At what year of age is the number of deaths greater?

According to insurance company averages, the number of deaths is greatest in the first year after birth. In 1961, there were 107,965 infant deaths reported in the United States. This was more than the number for each age from 1 through 55 years. A secondary peak in the number of deaths occurs near age 77.

134 Running Out Of Space
Great Britain became the first country in the world to have more cremations than burials. In Japan, it is said, graveyards are so crowded that only members of the imperial family are assured a resting place. West Berlin has had at least a six-week waiting period for burial. In Brazil, a 12-story "carneiro" has been built and there is a longstanding reservation.

Arlington National Cemetery is so crowded that officials are working on a columbarium to store 50,000 urns of ashes. Governments world-wide are worried that if people continue to die, soon no more places would be found to bury them.

135 Human Soul Weighs 21 Grams
A Swedish doctor in a new book says he discovered the human soul weighs 21 grams. He placed beds of terminal patients on sensitive scales and saw the needle drop when the patients died, he says.

—*Pastor's Manual*

136 . . . Except Taxes
Alisa Bonaparte as Napoleon's sister lay dying, someone in the room observed

that nothing was as certain as death. "Except taxes," added Alisa—thus making her last words among the most widely quoted in history.

—*Reader's Digest*

DEATHS, ATHEISTS

137 To Prefer Hell

Altamont the infidel, cried out his last words: "My principles have poisoned my friend; my extravagance has beggared my boy; my unkindness has murdered my wife. And is there another hell? Oh, thou blasphemed, yet most indulgent Lord God! Hell is a refuge if it hides me from thy frown."

138 So, It Is True!

A newspaper article referred to a striking story in an anonymous book of memoirs published not long ago. The writer met the woman who nursed the great agnostic, Professor J. H. Huxley, through his last illness. She said that as he lay dying the great skeptic suddenly looked up at some sight invisible to mortal eyes, and, staring a while, whispered at last, "So it *is* true."

—Reginald Kirby

139 Stalin's Terrible Death

Quoted in *Newsweek* is Svetlana Stalin's description of her father's death. We quote: "My father died a difficult and terrible death ... God grants an easy death only to the just .... At what seemed the very last moment he suddenly opened his eyes and cast a glance over everyone in the room. It was a terrible glance, insane or perhaps angry left hand as though he were pointing to something above and bringing down a curse on us all. The gesture was full of menace ... The next moment ... the spirit wrenched itself free of the flesh."

DEATHS, SAINTS

140 Aristeides Observed The Christians

About the year 125 A.D. a Greek by the name of Aristeides was writing to one of his friends about the new religion, Christianity. He was trying to explain the reasons for its extraordinary success. Here is a sentence from one of his letters:

"If any righteous man among the Christians passes from this world, they rejoice and offer thanks to God, and they escort his body with songs and thanksgiving as if he were setting out from one place to another nearby." •

—J. G. Gilkey

141 Moody More Alive

Realizing that he would soon be gone from this world one day, Moody said to a friend, "Someday you will read in the papers that D. L. Moody of Northfield is dead. Don't you believe a word of it.

"At that moment I shall be more alive than I am now. I shall have gone higher, that is all—out of this old clay tenement into a house that is immortal, a body that sin cannot touch, that sin cannot taint, a body fashioned into His glorious body. I was born in the flesh in 1837; I was born of the Spirit in 1856. That which is born of the flesh may die; that which is born of the Spirit will live forever."

142 Exchanging Soiled Banknote

Some said that death is paying a debt of nature. But it is not paying a debt, but rather exchanging money at the bank. We bring a crumpled note to the bank to obtain solid gold in exchange. In a Christian's death, you bring this cumbersome body, which you could not retain long; you lay it down and received for it, from the eternal treasures, liberty, victory, knowledge, rapture.

143 Lost?

A little girl whose baby brother had just died asked her mother where baby had gone. "To be with Jesus," replied the mother. A few days later, talking to a friend, the mother said, "I am so grieved to have lost my baby." The little girl heard her, and, remembering what her mother had told her, looked up into her and asked, "Mother, is a thing lost when you know where it is?"

"No, of course not." "Well, then, how can baby be lost when he has gone to be with Jesus?" Her mother never forgot this. It was the truth.

—*Junior King's Business*

144 Arrived!

There are Christians of a certain tribe in Africa who never say of their dead "who die in the Lord" that "they have departed!" Speaking, as it were, from the vantage point of the Gloryworld, they triumphantly and joyously say, "They have arrived!" What joy, even in sorrow, is our's when we say of our loved ones, who enter life eternal trusting Jesus. "Absent from the body—at home with the Lord!"

—Walter B. Knight

145 Called-Held-Kept!

Frances Havergal, the song writer, lived and moved in the Word of God. His Word was her constant companion. On the last day of her life, she asked a friend to read to her the 42nd chapter of Isaiah. When the friend read the sixth verse, "I the Lord have called thee in righteousness, and will hold thine hand, and will keep thee," Miss Havergal stopped her. She whispered, "Called—held—kept. I can go home on that!" And she did go home on that.

—*Pentecostal Evangel*

146 Benjamin Franklin's Epitaph

When Benjamin Franklin was about to die, he asked that a picture of Christ on the Cross should be so placed in his bedroom that he could look, as he said, "upon the form of the Silent Sufferer."

He wrote in advance the epitaph to be on his gravestone: "The body of Benjamin Franklin, Printer, like the cover of an old book, its contents torn out and stripped of its lettering and gilding, lies here . . . Yet the Work itself shall not be lost; for it will, as he believed, appear once more in a new and more beautiful edition, corrected and amended by the Author."

147 Epigram

●Those who love God never meet for the last time.   —W. G. Elmslie

●Death is not a period but a comma in the story of life.   —Amos J. Tarver,
in Christian Herald

●At a funeral service in Winona Lake, Indiana: "We are not in the land of the living, but in the land of the dying—someday we shall be in the Land of the Living."

●No one cries when children, long absent from their parents, go home. School is out. It is time to go home. Vacation morning is a happy occasion.

—Beecher

●"We go to the grave of a friend, saying, "A man is dead." But angels throng about him saying, "A man is born."

●The Christian, at his death, should not be like the child who is forced by the rod to quit his play, but like one who is wearied of it and is willing to go home.

—Gotthold

●When I go down to the grave I can say, like so many others: I have finished my work, but I cannot say I have finished my life. My day's work will begin the next morning. My tomb is not a blind alley. It is a thoroughfare. It closes in the twilight to open in the dawn.   —Victor Hugo

●An aged Scotchman, while dying, was asked what he thought of death, and he replied, "It matters little to me whether I live or die. If I die I will be with Jesus, and if I live Jesus will be with me."
— A. C. Dixon

●Death did not first strike Adam, the first sinful man; nor Cain, the first murderer: but Abel, the innocent and righteous.
— Bishop Hall

DECEIT

148 "Blind" Man Goes To Movies

President Walter G. Clippinger of Otterbein College in Ohio, enjoys the story of the fake blind man.

The pitiable creature, with dark glasses and his little tin cup was standing on the street corner, patiently waiting for some small contribution. A kindly man passed by and generously dropped a dime in the poor old fellow's cup. Then for some reason he turned around, and to his surprise saw the blind man's glasses pushed up on his forehead, and his eager eyes closely examining the recent gift.

"I thought you were a blind man," said the disgruntled donor.

"Oh. no," was the answer, "I am only substituting for the regular blind man today. I'm not really blind at all."

"Well, where is the regular blind man?" asked the other.

"Oh, he's gone to the movies; it's his afternoon off."

149 Imaginary General In Action

During the Balkan wars that preceded World War I. McAlister Coleman was a war correspondent for the New York Sun. Only slightly handicapped by the fact that the paper's budget would not cover overseas travel, Coleman simply created a "General" who went on winning battles all over the map.

Other papers, bemoaning the Sun's scoops, sent their reporters to the battlefields to locate this victorious General. Finally, when Mac realized other reporters were getting too closely to where his "general" was located, he killed off his hero in a final blaze of glory.

150 Starting Early

A little boy was lost during the Christmas shopping rush. He was standing in an aisle of the busy department store crying, "I want my mommy." People kept passing by, giving the unhappy youngster nickels and dimes.

Finally a floorwalker came over to him and said, "I know where your mommy is, son." The little boy looked up with his teardrenched eyes and said, "So do I ... just keep quiet!"
— Pastor's Manual

DEDICATION

151 Pliny's Testimony

Pliny, governor of Bithynia, wrote Trajan the Emperor regarding how he flush out Christians in his area: "I gave these men chance to invoke the gods of Rome, offer sacrifice to the image of the Emperor, and finally to curse the name of Christ," adding "none of these acts, those who are really Christians can be forced to do."

152 Resolutions Of College President

At age 19, these resolutions were adopted by Dr. James Clement Furman, first president of Furman University, and are appropriate on every observance of Founder's Day at Furman University.

"Resolved, never to speak ill of an individual but to call to mind my own sins and imperfections and be silent.

"Resolved, when my heart feels cold and languid, to strive earnestly in prayer to God for deliverance from such a state and for the abiding influence of His Holy Spirit; and to enquire into the causes which have produced this effect upon me and to guard against them in the future.

"Resolved, never to go to bed without having endeavored to learn something more of God as He is revealed in the Holy Scriptures than I knew when I rose in the morning.

"Resolved, to keep in mind during the business of the day the good resolutions which I may have formed for my assistance so that if I neglect them, I may humble myself and in my retirement earnestly seek pardon from God.

"Resolved, to say nothing to irritate the feelings of anyone and especially of my relations and friends.

"Resolved, to leave as soon as possible any company which might draw off my thoughts from the things of eternity.

"Resolved, never to neglect to devote a certain portion of every twenty-four hours to secret meditation and prayer.

"Resolved, never to halt in doing anything of which I am convinced that it is duty."

—Selected

153 Handel's Messiah Is Born

When Handel composed "The Messiah," for twenty-three days he completely withdrew from the things of this world. So immersed was he in his music that the food brought to him was often left untouched. Describing his feeling when the "Hallejah Chorus" burst on his mind, Handel said, "I did think I did see all Heaven before me, and the great God Himself."

—J. B. Dengis

DIETING

154 Obesity In US

Obesity is one of the most common medical complaints in the US today. About one-tenth to one-quarter of the US population is overweight to some extent, and spends over $400 million a year on reducing drugs and treatments. Physicians interested in this area of practice have even formed the American Society of Bariatrics.

155 Diet Soft Drinks

Bottlers sell $1.5 billion worth of diet soft drinks annually. That is 15% of the total U.S. soft-drink market, and has been the fastest growing segment, thanks to heavy advertising and a weight-conscious citizenry.

156 Fat People's Policy

People who go on a diet can now have another tangible measure of their progress: life-insurance rates that trim down along with their waistlines. Under a new program, members of Weight Watchers International, Inc., the firm that has some 3,000,000 members, are given these incentives:

Premiums for term life-insurance policies are based not only on age but also on bulk. Members who lose the required number of pounds and keep them off for at least six months are given rate reductions.

Previously, the most cholesterol-clogged division pay about four times the premium assessed on people of the same age who have reached the weights. Thus the cost of an eating spree can now be measure in cash as well as calories.

157 Fattest Men

It appears that people are getting fatter as the centuries roll by—at least for the heavyweight record holders.

During the 18th century, Edward Bright of Essex, England, was fat enough to be recorded in books. His weight was 616 pounds. He died in 1750, age thirty.

In 1857, Miles Darden came along,

weighing slightly over 1,000 lbs. He was the heaviest man then known to medical science.

Then Robert Earl Hughes was born in Monticello, Illinois in 1926. This 11½ lb. baby weighted 203 lbs. at age 6,

378 lbs. at age 10,
546 lbs. at age 13,
693 lbs. at age 18,
896 lbs. at age 25,
945 lbs. at age 27,
1,041 lbs. at age 32 when he died.

His greatest recorded weight was 1,069 lbs. His coffin was as large as a piano case, and had to be lowered by crane.

DISCIPLESHIP

158 "Ready For Either"

"Ready for Either" is the significant legend that underspans the seal of the Baptist Missionary Union, which presents an ox standing with a plough on one side, and an altar on the other.

159 How Each Apostle Died

All of the apostles were insulted by the enemies of their Master. They were called to seal their doctrines with their blood and nobly did they bear the trial.

Matthew suffered martyrdom by being slain with a sword at a distant city of Ethiopia.

Mark expired at Alexandria, after being cruelly dragged through the streets of that city.

Luke was hanged upon an olive tree in the classic land of Greece.

John was put in a caldron of boiling oil, but escaped death in a miraculous manner, and was afterward branded at Patmos.

Peter was crucified at Rome with his head downward.

James, the Greater, was beheaded at Jerusalem,

James, the Less, was thrown from a

lofty pinnacle of the temple, and then beaten to death with a fuller's club.

Bartholomew was flayed alive.

Andrew was bound to a cross, whence he preached to his persecutors until he died.

Thomas was run through the body with a lance at Coromandel in the East Indies.

Jude was shot to death with arrows.

Matthias was first stoned and then beheaded.

Barnabas of the Gentiles was stoned to death at Salonica.

Paul, after various tortures and persecutions, was at length beheaded at Rome by the Emperor Nero.

Such was the fate of the apostles, according to traditional statements.

—*Christian Index*

160 God Can Do It

Longfellow could take a worthless sheet of paper, write a poem on it, and make it worth $6,000—*that's genius.*

Rockefeller could sign his name to a piece of paper and make it worth million dollars—*that's capital.*

Uncle Sam can take gold, stamp an eagle on it, and make it worth $20.00 *that's money.*

A mechanic can take material that is worth only $5.00 and make it worth $50.00—*that's skill.*

An artist can take a fifty-cent piece of canvas, paint a picture on it, and make it worth $1.000—*that's art.*

God can take a worthless, sinful life, wash it in the blood of Christ, put His Spirit in it, and make it a blessing to humanity— *that's salvation.*

—*Christian Digest*

161 Stomping On The Violin

It was advertised in one of our large cities that a great violinist would play on a violin worth $6,000. The theatre was packed. Many were curious and wanted to hear such an expensive instrument being played. The violinist went on stage and played very beautifully.

Suddenly, he threw the violin on the floor and then began to stomp on it, crushing it to pieces, then walked off the stage. The people were shocked. But then the manager came on stage and said that the violinist did not really use the $1,000 violin but a $20 one. He would now play on the $1,000 one. And so he did. But few people could tell the difference. He simply wanted to show that it was the violinist rather than the violin that makes the music.

In the Master's hands, even a $20 fiddle would make good music.

162 We Have A King!

The Spaniards were besieging the little town of St. Quentin, on the frontiers of France. Its ramparts were in ruins; fever and famine were decimating its defenders; treason existed among its terrified population. One day the Spaniards shot over the walls a shower of arrows, to which were attached little slips of parchment, promising the inhabitants that if they would surrender, their lives and property would be spared.

The governor of the town was the great leader of the Huguenots, Gaspard de Coligni. As his sole answer he took a piece of parchment, tied it to a javelin, wrote on it the two words Regem habemus—"We have a king!"—and hurled it back into the camp of the enemy. There was his one answer to all their threats and all their enducements.

163 Rudolph's Master

There was once a young man in old Vienna named Rudolph. He determined one day to write a symphony; he set to work and labored hard; he wrote it and rewrote it. Then he called in some friends and went over it with them; they were loud in their praises. They said: "It's great,

Rudolph; it will make you a great name." But he wasn't satisfied with it. He went over it again and again until at last he had finished it. Then he set the orchestra to work upon it.

Finally the night came when it was to be given to the public. The great hall was literally packed with people, and as the beauties of the harmony floated out over then it touched a responsive chord in their lives, it melted their hearts and they caught the inspiration of the composer. When the last strain had died out there was a moment's silence, then the great throng went almost wild in the demonstration of their enthusiasm, and hundreds flocked to the stage to congratulate the young musician.

But he stood there unmoved. After the crowd had passed away somewhat, there came down the aisle an old whitehaired man. Going up to the young man, he placed both his hands on his shoulders and said, "It was well done, Rudolph, it was well done." Then it was that a smile of satisfaction stole over the face of the young musician. That was his master.

—E. A. Krapp

DIVORCES

164 Divorce Statistics

In 1976, 2,133,000 marriage licenses were issued in the United States—and 1,077,000 divorces were granted. A ratio now of 1 to 2!

The US Census Bureau gave the following figures:

*In 1920, 1 divorce for every 7 marriages

*In 1940, 1 divorce for every 6 marriages

*In 1960, 1 divorce for every 4 marriages

*In 1972, 1 divorce for every 3 marriages

More frightening, it is estimated that as

early as 1990, divorces will outnumber marriages.

165 Family Of 28 Children Divorced

From an Atlantic City courtroom emerged this unusual story. True, the wife had deserted her husband, but it was a "wholesale" desertion.

The Italian husband was originally a widower with 17 children. She, also Italian, was originally a widow with 11 children. The wedding made a combined family of 28 children. But it was not one big happy family. Mrs. De Parsio finally deserted her husband, taking her 11 children on a truck one night and headed towards Philadelphia. This left Mr. De Parsio with his original 17 children. The number of broken lives!

E

EARTHQUAKES

166 Total Quakes Annually
Every year. there are some 500,000 detectable seismic or micro-seismic disturbances around the world. Of these. 100.000 can be felt and 1.000 cause some damage.

167 Record Of Increasing Quakes
In the 9th century. there was one major earthquakes; in the 11th century, two; in the 13th century. three; in the 16th; two; 17th. two; 18th. five (including the Lisbon); and in the 19th century. nine major earthquakes. So far in the 20th century. there have been over 40 (including the Peking quake).

From the *World Almanac* comes another set of facts: there were only 6 earthquakes of strength between 1800 to 1896. But in each decade from 1897 until 1947. there were either 2 or 3. and in the decade from 1947 to 1956. there were 7. From 1957 to 1966. there were 17.

Time magazine's front cover for its Sept. 1. 1975 issue was a split earth with this inscription: "FORECAST: EARTH-QUAKE." Since that date to the end of 1976. there have been 24 significant earthquakes—in China. Guatemala, Italy, Indonesia. Soviet Central Asia, and many other places.

The year 1976 experienced at least 50 significant quakes (intensity 6.5) and 18 major quakes (over 7.0). An estimated 695.000 deaths—the highest in modern history—in 1976 were reported by the US Geological Survey.

EDUCATION, RELIGIOUS

168 Christian Schools Enrollments
Enrollments in fulltime Protestant schools rose 20% from 2,992,000 to 3,000,-000 in 1976. Fulltime Catholic schools went down 38% from 5.6 million in 1966 to 3.5 million in 1976. Fulltime Jewish school enrollment went up 37% from 60.000 in 1966 to 82,000 in 1976.

169 Bible School Enrollment Is Up
In 1975. the number of students in secular universities fell by 14%, but. for Bible colleges it jumped 7.5%.

ETERNITY

170 The Googol

No matter how large a number is. it is finite: it is always possible to mention a number that is larger. Scientists speak of the "googol." It is a one. followed by 100 zeros. The googol is inconceivably large. But then think of the "googolplexes" which we believe is the googol raised to the googol-th power." It is said. that if this number were written out. there would not be space on earth to contain the pages required. In fact. they would more than fill our galaxy!

—*Christian Victory*

171 Eternity's Single Day

High up in the North. in the land called Svithjod. there stands a rock. It is 100 miles high and 100 miles wide. Once every 1000 years a little bird comes to this rock to sharpen its break. When the rock has thus been worn away. then a single day of eternity will have gone by.

—Hendrick Willen Van Loon

172 "Immortality" Too Short?

At a meeting of the Presbyterian General Assembly. the moderator announced: "The next number will be an address by Rev. James McCosh. Chancellor of Princeton University. Subject: 'The immortality of the Soul.' Time allotted: Fifteen minutes."

—Maxwell Droke

EUROPE

173 Prophecy of European Union

Dr. Walter Hallstein. former president of the European Economic Community said:

"Three phases of the European unification are to be noted. First. the customs union, second. the economic union, third. the political union . . .what we have created on the way to uniting Europe is a mighty economic-political union of which nothing may be sacrificed for any reason. Its value exists not only in what it is. but more in what it promises to become... At about 1980 we may fully expect the great fusion of all economic. military. and political communities together into the United States of Europe."

174 Most Militarized Region

The European continent is one of the world's most heavily militarized regions. The Western allies have 1.175.000 men under arms, including 208.500 Americans in West Germany. The Warsaw Pact has 1.305.000 troops. of whom 775.000 are Russians. Both sides have ultramodern weapons, including nuclear weapons.

175 Advantages In European Unity

If the Europeans should unite. the federation will:
*have 253 million people
*be 23% more populous than the U.S.
*be more productive than the USSR
*have control over more of the world's trade than the US and Japan combined
*have 2.450.000 men under arms—almost as many as China.

EVANGELICALS

176 Phenomenon Of 1970s

For the first time in United States history. most major church denominations stopped growing and began to shrink—except the conservative denominations! Census of churches reveal that conservative bodies invariably move to the top of any growth listings. while National Council (liberal) churches occupy lower positions. The RULE: the most ecumenical and liberal the denomination, the more membership losses it suffers. Examples of exceptional growths are the Southern Baptists (which saw a Baptist to the White House in 1977), the Assemblies of God, the Church of the Nazarene, and others.

Five theological schools now rank ahead of the liberal Union Theological Seminary, which had held the no. 1 spot for most of its 140 years — Dallas Theological, Fuller Theological, Gordon-Conwell Theological, Asbury Theological, and Trinity Divinity Seminary. All these growing schools uphold the historical accuracy and inspiration of Scripture. The more rigidly conservative, the larger its growth!

177 One In Three "Born Again"

One in three adult Americans say they've been "born again," according to recent Gallup Poll. Half (51%) all Protestants polled, 18% Roman Catholics, claimed conversion experience for close to 50 million total. Gallup listed literal interpretation of Scripture, belief that one must witness as marks of evangelical: four in ten nationwide (38%), 46% Protestants, 31% Catholics hold that view of Scripture; 47% nationally said they had asked others to believe in Christ.

178 Criswell's Appeal

We have referred in these pages at various times to Dr. W. A. Criswell, pastor of the 15,000-member First Baptist Church of Dallas, Texas. When he was President of the Southern Baptist Convention, he issued an appeal to the liberals in the denomination to leave the ranks of the Southern Baptists and to start their own denomination.

Although the conservatives are by far

the more numerous and vocal camp in the SBC, they can invoke no doctrinal discipline to block the liberals' inroad.

179 Moody Bible Institute Dedicated

When Dwight L. Moody was dedicating the first building of what later became the Moody Bible Institute, he gave the cornerstone a whack with the trowel, then made an invocation to this effect: 'Lord, you know that what this old world needs more than anything else is thy Word. We pray that if the day ever comes when anything contrary to the Bible is taught here, you will wipe this school from the face of the earth."

—*Sunday School Times*

EVOLUTIONISTS

180 The Evolution Theory

As taught in our public schools today, the Organic Theory of Evolution accounts for the origin of mankind as follows:

"Life on this planet originated several billion years ago, when electrical disturbances caused reactions to occur in the chemicals of the primeval ocean, and these reactions produced amino acids, and these amino acids organized themselves into living cells. As time went on, more chemical reactions caused the descendants of these one-called organisms to mutate and develop into a variety of types of multi-celled plants and animals.

"The process continued, and as each new variety of organism appeared, natural selection would result in its being either better or less suited to the environment, and therefore it would either flourish or disappear. In the long run, then, species of plants and animals better and better suited to their respective environments appeared and developed.

"Man is the highest product of this

development. He is immediately descended from the same ancestors as the apes; more remotely, from the same ancestors as all mammals. He is himself still developing; that process is stalled by our present lifestyle, but biologically it is inevitable."

— *The Bible Friend*

181 "It Appears That" Etc.

The theory of the evolution of man is based on suppositions and inferences. As an example, the first chapter of Charles Darwin's book *The Descent of Man* contains within a few pages, 20 expressions of uncertainty, such as "seemed," "it appears," "take for granted," "may," and implies." The concluding chapter of 14 pages has more than 50 such expressions. Within 30 years after publication the book was changed in 87 places.

—Elizabeth A. Schroeter

182 In The Beginning, God

The ancient Egyptians believed that a flat world rested on four pillars of stone and the ancient Hindus believed that a flat world rested on the back of a huge elephant, the elephant stood on the back of an enormous turtle, and the turtle stood on an immense coiled snake!

Instead of promulgating such puerile theories, Moses, who was educated in Egyptian schools, but who was inspired by God to write the creation account in Genesis, gave us the true, God breathed account, in words of grand simplicity, matchless beauty and exquisite accuracy: "In the beginning God created the heaven and the earth."

—Fred J. Meldan

183 Literal Interpretation of Gen. 1

The "recent creation" view of Genesis 1, we think, has the strongest merits. It has the following foundational observations:

(1) Heaven and earth were created in six literal days. There is no interval between Gen. 1:1 and 1:2.

(2) The earth was created "empty and void" in the sense that no life and no outstanding features, such as hills, valleys, were visible.

(3) Satan's fall occurred after the creation of Adam and Eve. Gen. 1:31; Rom. 5:12.

(4) Fossils came into existence at the time of Noah's Flood. Gen. 6-9 recorded an universal catastrophe.

(5) Earth is probably not older than 10,000 years. Rocks and earth-materials were created "of age." Man and animals were not millions of years in origin but of relatively similar years.

EXPECTATION, SPIRIT OF

184 Minimizing Future Shock

Pastor D. Leroy Sanders of the 2,000-member First Assembly of God in North Hollywood, California, believes in having everything in order in the event of an emergency. Like, the Second Coming, Sanders and his people believes that when that happens they will suddenly disappear (be raptured) from the earth. But what about afterward—what would happen to the $1.5 million church property, and how could the possibly remaining members keep the church operating?

Sanders took his questions to attorneys and denominational officials. Result: the church unanimously agreed to change its by-laws providing for a "temporary chairman" and election of new officers when the event occurs. To finance the work, members have been urged to rewrite their wills and insurance policies, naming the church as beneficiary. And to minimize initial confusion, the mortgage company has been alerted to the expected emergency, and consultations are underway with a major insurance company to determine how claims may be paid without waiting the usual seven-year period for missing person.

—Selected

185 "Perhaps Today"

Dr. Horatius Bonar, as he drew the curtains at night and retired to rest, used to repeat to himself the words, as if in prayer, and certainly with expectancy, 'Perhaps tonight, Lord!' In the morning, as he awoke and looked out on the dawn of a new day, he would say, looking up into the sky, 'Perhaps today, Lord!' He expected the Lord to return at any moment. Bonar was in the Lord's service

for over 60 years.

—A. Naismith

186 Witness From Our Capitol's Dome

There is an inscription in the dome of our Capitol in Washington which few people know about. It says: "One far-off divine event toward which the whole creation moves." A visitor saw this inscription and asked the guide what it meant. he said: "I think it refers to the second coming of Christ." When the dome of our Capitol was erected. some God-fearing official ordered that inscription to be etched in the dome of our seat of government. believing that its truth was vital to the concern of our nation.

—Billy Graham

F

FAITH

187 Pulling On Both Oars

An old Scotsman operated a little rowboat for transporting passengers. One day a passenger noticed that the good old man had carved on one oar the word "Faith." and on the other oar the word "Works." Curiosity led him to ask the meaning of this. The old man, being a well-balanced Christian and glad of the opportunity for testimony, said, "I will show you."

So saying, he dropped one oar and plied the other called Works, and they just went around in circles. Then he dropped that oar and began to ply the oar called Faith, and the little boat just went around in circles again — this time the other way around, but still in a circle.

After this demonstration the old man picked up Faith and Works, and plying both oars together, sped swiftly over the water, explaining to his inquiring passenger, "You see, that is the way it is in the Christian life. Dead works without faith are useless, and 'faith without works is dead' also, getting you nowhere. But faith and works pulling together make for safety, progress, and blessing."

—*Bible Friend*

188 Umbrellas And Faith

A colored church congregation had met to pray for rain to release a long dry spell. The preacher looked severely at his flock and said:

"Brothers and Sisters, yo'll knows why we is here. Now what I wants to know is—where is yo' umbrellas?"

189 Epigram

●Faith sees the invisible, believes the incredible, and receives the impossible.

●Faith is to accept the impossible, do without the indispensable, and bear the intolerable.

●Faith is idle when circumstances are right, only when they are adverse is one's faith in God exercised. Faith, like muscle, grows strong and supple with exercise.

●Don't be afraid to take a big step if one is indicated. You can't cross a chasm in two small jumps.

—David Lloyd George

●A little faith will bring your soul to

heaven; a great faith will bring heaven to your soul. —Spurgeon

●Faith is not believing that God *can*, but that God. *will!*

●Faith is to believe what we do not see; and the reward of this faith is to see what we believe.

●Faith in God is indispensable to successful statesmanship.

—Abraham Lincoln

FAITHFULNESS

190 As Usual With Wesley

A lady once asked John Wesley that suppose he were to know that he would die at 12:00 midnight tomorrow, how would he spend the intervening time. His reply: "Why madam, just as I intend to spend it now. I would preach this evening at Gloucester, and again at five tomorrow morning; after that I would ride to Tewkesbury, preach in the afternoon, and meet the societies in the evening. I would then go to rend Martin's house, who expects to entertain me, talk and pray with the family as usual, retire to my room at 10 o'clock, commend myself to my heavenly Father, lie down to rest, and wake up in Glory."

191 King Practices Obedience

It is said of Henry of Bavaria that at one time, becoming weary of court life, he determined to enter a monastery. When he presented himself to Prior Richard, the faithful monk gave him the strict rules of the order. The king listened eagerly and enthusiastically expressed pleasure at the prospect of such complete consecration.

Then the prior insisted that obedience, implicit and expressed was the first requisite of sainthood. The monarch promised to follow his will in every detail. "Then go back to your throne and do your duty in the station God assigned you," was the prior's word to him. The king took up his scepter again, and from then until he died, his people said of him, "King Henry has learned to govern by learning to obey."

—The Treasury

192 Two Costliest Words

King Joao V of Portugal paid almost one-fourth of a billion dollars during the 18th century for the two words "REI FIDELISSIMO" (Most Faithful King). In exchange for this exorbitant sum, the king won the right to display these two words in his title.

This extravaganza however exhausted all the wealth Portugal had extracted from Brazil up to then. And when the king died, having no money in the treasury to bury him decently, a public collection had to be taken for his burial.

193 One Year To Live

The *Baltimore Sun* conducted a contest, and the following poem received a prize for the best answer to the question, "What would you do if you had one more year to live?"

"If I had but one year to live;
One year to help; one year to give;
One year to love; one year to bless;
One year of better things to stress;
One year to sing; one year to smile;
To brighten earth a little while;
One year to sing my Maker's praise;
One year to fill with work my days;
One year to strive for a reward
When I should stand before my Lord.

I think that I would spend each day,
In just the very self-same way
That I do now. For from afar
The call may come across the bar
At any time, and I must be
Prepared to meet eternity.
So if I have a year to live,

Or just one day in which to give
A pleasant smile, a helping hand.
A mind that tries to understand
A fellow-creature when in need;
'Tis one with me—I take no heed.
But try to live each day He sends
To serve my gracious Master's ends."
— Mary Davis Reed

FAMILY

194 Carter Urges More Family Life

Top White House staff personnel were urged in a handwritten memorandum from President Jimmy Carter to spend "an adequate amount of time" with their families to assure a stable family life. Written on White House stationery and signed "J. Carter," the memorandum says:

"I am concerned about the family lives of all of you. I want you to spend an adequate amount of time with your husbands, wives, and children, and also to involve them as much as possible in our White House life. We are going to be here a long time, and all of you will be more valuable to me and the country with rest and a stable home life. In emergencies we'll all work full time. Let me have your comments."

195 If Jesus Came To Your House

If Jesus came to your house to spend a
  day or two . . . .
If He came unexpectedly, I wonder
  what you'd do.
Oh, I know you'd give your nicest
  room to such an honored guest
And all the food you'd serve to Him
  would be the very best,
And you would keep assuring Him
  you're glad to have Him there . . . .
But . . . . when you saw Him coming,
  would you meet Him at the door
With arms outstretched in welcome to
  our heav'nly visitor?
Or would you maybe change your
  clothes before you let Him in,

Or hide some magazines and put the
  Bible where they'd been?
Would you turn off the radio and hope
  He hadn't heard,
And wish you hadn't uttered that last,
  loud and hasty word?
Would you hide your worldly music
  and put some hymn books out?
Could you let Jesus walk right in, or
  would you rush about?
And I wonder . . . . If the Savior spent a
  day or two with you,
Would you go right on doing the things
  you always do?
Would you go right on saying the
  things you always say?
Would life for you continue as it does
  from day to day?
Would your family conversation keep
  up its usual pace?
And would you find it hard each meal
  to say a table grace?
Would you sing the songs you always
  sing and read the book you read?
And let Him know the things on
  which your mind and spirit feed
Would you take Jesus with you everywhere you'd planned to go,
Or would you, maybe, change your
  plans for just a day or so?
Would you be glad to have Him meet
  your very closest friends,
Or would you hope they'd stay away
  until His visit ends?
Would you be glad to have Him stay
  for-ever on and on,
Or would you sigh with great relief
  when He at last was gone?
It might be interesting to know the
  things that you would do,
If Jesus came in person to spend some
  time with you.
— Author Unknown

196 The Christian Home

How God must love a friendly home
  Which has a warming smile,

63

To welcome everyone who comes
　　To bide a little while!
How God must love a happy home
　　Where song and laughter show,
Hearts full of joyous certainty
　　That life means ways to grow!

How God must love a loyal home
　　Serenely sound and sure!
When troubles come to those within,
　　They still can feel secure.

How God must love a Christian home
　　Where faith and love attest
That every moment, every hour,
　　He is the honored Guest!
　　　　　　— *The Pentecostal Messenger*

197 Beauty Of A House

The beauty of a house is harmony,
The security of a house is loyalty,
The joy of a house is love,
The plenty of a house is in children,
The rule of a house is service,
The comfort of a house is God Him-
　　self.
　　　　　　　　　　— Frank Crane

198 Epigram

●All happy families are alike, but each
unhappy family is unhappy in its own
way.　　　　　　　　　— Leo Tolstoy

●Most homes nowadays seem to be on
three shifts. Father is on the night shift;
mother is on the day shift, and the
children shift for themselves.

●One per cent of the child's time is
spent under the influence of the Sunday
school; 7 per cent under the influence of
the public school; 92 per cent under the
influence of the home.
　　　　　　　　— Albert S. Taylor

●A 5 year-old to friend: "My father
can beat your father."
Reply: "So can my mother."

FATHER

199 Three Hairs And Lost Influence

A strange dog came to a preacher's
house, and his three sons soon became
quite fond of it. It so happened that there
were three white hairs in the animal's tail.
One day an advertisement was seen in the
newspaper about a lost dog which fitted
that description perfectly. "In the presence of my three boys," said the minister,
"we carefully separated the three white
hairs and removed them." The real owner
discovered where the straying canine had
found a home and came to claim him. The
dog showed every sign of recognition, so
the man was ready to take him away.

Quickly the minister spoke up, "Didn't
you say the dog would be known by three
white hairs in its tail?" The owner, unable to find the identifying feature, was
forced to leave. The minister said later,
"we kept the dog, but I lost my three boys
for Christ." His sons no longer had confidence in what their father professed. He
hadn't practiced what he preached.
　　　　　　　　— *Our Daily Bread*

200 "The Day We Visited Our
　　　Son's Tomb"

O New York, O Brooklyn, O Cypress
　　Hills!
At last we found the tomb of our son!
Amidst heavy rains and spring chills,
We can't help but let our tears run.

Today we come from thousands of miles
　　away,
With trembling hands, I plant chry-
　　santhemums on the soil;
While your Ma, brother, and sisters sob-
　　bingly pray,
I recall how your childhood days were
　　spoiled.

We all missed you for more than one and
　　a half years,
Each day I think of you twenty odd times;
Countless occasions did I secretly shed

tears,
Terribly missed is when morning sun climbs!

Ah graveyards, more graveyards we come across!
They are old ages, ancients, and horrors;
You are so young, promising, and robust,
Why select all these as your neighbors?

Day and night you are wandering here as an alien soul,
By great continents and oceans we are far segregated;
When is the day your ashes we may retrieve and haul
Back to Loyola where your new tomb has been erected?

—C.B. Lim

NOTE: Mr. C.B. Lim is a close friend of the author. His son was killed in a taxi accident in New York City while journeying from the Philippines to Canada.

201 An Old Soldier's Prayer

"Build me a son, O Lord, who will be strong enough to know when he is weak, and brave enough to face himself when he is afraid; one who will be proud and unbending in honest defeat, and humble and gentle in victory.

"Build me a son whose wishes will not take the place of deeds; a son who will know Thee ... and that to know himself is the foundation stone of knowledge.

"Build me a son whose heart will be clear, whose goal will be high, a son who will master himself before he seeks to master other men one who will reach into the future, yet never forget the past.

"And after all these things are his, add, I pray, enough of a sense of humor, so that he may always be serious, yet never take himself too seriously. Give him humility, so that he may always remember the simplicity of true greatness, the open mind of true wisdom and the meekness of true strength.

"Then I, his father, will dare to whisper, 'I have not lived in vain'."
—Gen Douglas A. MacArthur

202 Father's Day Flower

The official flower on Father's Day is the dandelion, because the more it is trampled upon, the better it grows.

203 Penny's Father Didn't Laugh

If it had not been for a crooked groceryman, J.C. Penney might have become the owner of a grocery store rather than the owner of a dry goods chain and the nation's leading merchandiser.

When he was a teenager, Jim worked for a groceryman in Hamilton, Missouri. He liked the work and had plans to make a career of it. One night he came home and proudly told his family about his "foxy" employer. The grocer had a practice of mixing low quality coffee with the expensive brand and thus increasing his profit. Jim laughed as he told the story at the supper table.

His father didn't see anything funny about the practice. "Tell me," he said, "if the grocer found someone palming off an inferior article on him for the price of the best, do you think he would think they were just being foxy, and laugh about it?"

Jim could see his father was disappointed in him. "I guess not," he replied. "I guess I just didn't think about it that way."

Jim's father instructed him to go to the grocer the next day and collect whatever money due him and tell the grocer he wouldn't be working for him any longer. Jobs were not plentiful in Hamilton, but Mr. Penney would rather his son be unemployed than be associated with a crooked businessman.

J.C. Penney came that close to becoming a grocer.

FELLOWSHIP

204 Blest Be The Ties That Bind

In 1765 John Fawcett was called to pastor a very small congregation at Wainsgate, England. He labored there diligently for 7 years, but his salary was so meager that he and his wife could scarcely obtain the necessities of life. Though the people were poor, they compensated for this lack by their faithfulness and warm fellowship.

Then Dr. Fawcett received a call from a much larger church in London, and after lengthy consideration decided to accept the invitation. As his few possesions were being placed in a wagon for moving, many of his parishioners came to say goodby. Once again they pleaded with him to reconsider.

Touched by this great outpouring of love, he and his wife began to weep. Finally Mrs. Fawcett exclaimed, "O John, I just can't bear this. They need us so badly here." "God has spoken to my heart, too!" he said. "Tell them to unload the wagon! We cannot break these wonderful ties of fellowship."

This experience inspired Fawcett to write a hymn. "Blest be the tie that binds our hearts in Christian love! The fellowship of kindred mind is like to that above."

—H.G. Bosch

205 Livingstone's Encouragement

The first attempt of David Livingstone to preach ended in failure: "Friends, I have forgotten all I had to say," he gasped, and in shame stepped from the pulpit!

At that moment, Robert Moffat who was visiting Edinburgh advised David not to give up. Perhaps he could be a doctor instead of a preacher, he advised. Livingstone decided to be both. When the years of medical study were done, he went to Africa.

206 Lesson From The Bees

One bee always seem ready to feed another bee, sometimes even one of a different colony. Mutual feeding among bees, who are very social insects, is the order of their existence. The workers feed the helpless queen who cannot feed herself. They feed the drones during their period of usefulness in the hive. Of course they feed the young. They seem to enjoy the social act.

Bees cluster together for warmth in cold weather and fan their wings to cool the hive in hot weather, thus working for one another's comfort.

When swarming time comes, bee scouts take out to find suitable quarters where the new colony can establish itself. These scouts report back to the group, executing a dance (as they also do to report honey) by which they convey the location of the prospective home to the colony. As more than one scout goes prospecting and reports back, the bees appear to entertain the findings of all scouts and at last the entire assembly seems to reach a common conclusion on a choice. Thereupon they all take wing in what is called a swarm.

—Virginia Whitman

FLATTERY

207 Electronic Applause

The Pacific Organ Studios on Clement Street is selling something that might lessen man's insecurity. It's an organ called the Chamberlain Music Master, which includes a button that delivers, via tape, a round of applause "of concert-hall size." You play "Chop-sticks," press the applause button and bask in the distant patter of 2000 paws. Think what this does for the ego.

—San Francisco *Chronicle*

208 "You're Beautiful"

The telephone company in an English city is planning a service known as MOR (for Morale). When Dad goes off to work in a huff or forgets a birthday or yells at the kids, Mom can run to the phone, dial MOR and hear a soothing male voice coo: "You're quite, quite beautiful, you know."

—Alton, Ill., *Telegraph*

209 Capitalizing On John Smiths

John Smith is still the most common name in this country. It was for that reason that Mark Twain dedicated his story of *The Celebrated Jumping Frog* to John Smith. "who I have known in diverse and sundry places and whose many and manifold virtues did always command my esteem."

Twain figured that anyone to whom a book is dedicated would be sure to buy at least one copy, and since there were thousands of John Smiths, his book would be assured of at least a modest sale.

—*Bits & Pieces*

210 Pastor Watches Own Funeral

Fort Lauderdale, Florida (AP)—The Rev. Ivory W. Mizell commemorated his 64th birthday by watching his own funeral. "I think it was good. It was much better than I expected." he said after Wednesday night's service at the first Baptist Church of Piney Grove.

On the programs printed up for the service were these words: "This, my funeral service, is being held because I have no pleasure in words I cannot hear, flowers I cannot smell and friends I cannot see."

FORGIVING

211 Inability To Think

In a recent chapel service bulletin from Chaplain Wendell C. Hawley, comes a classic illustration of forgiveness. When the Moravian missionaries first went to the Eskimos, they could not find a word in their language for forgiveness, so they had to compound one. This turned out to be: Issumagijoujungnainermik. It is a formidable looking assembly of letters, but an expression that has a beautiful connotation for those who understand it. It means: "Not-being-able-to-think-about-it-anymore."

—*Minister' Research Service*

212 Success On "The Last Supper"

Leonardo da Vinci was one of the outstanding intellects of all history, for he was great as a draftsman, an engineer,and a thinker. Just before he commenced work on his "Last Supper" he had a violent quarrel with a fellow painter. So enraged and bitter was Leonardo that he determined to paint the face of his enemy, the other artist, into the face of Judas, and thus take his revenge and vent his spleen by handling the man down in infamy and scorn to succeeding generations. The face of Judas was therefore one of the first that he finished, and everyone could easily recognize it as the face of the painter with whom he had quarreled.

But when he came to paint the face of Christ, he could make no progress. Something seemed to be baffling him, holding him back, frustrating his best efforts. At length he came to the conclusion that the thing which was checking and frustrating him was the fact that he had painted his enemy into the face of Judas. He therefore painted out the face of Judas and commenced anew on the face of Jesus, and this time with the success which the ages have acclaimed.

You cannot at one and the same time be painting the features of Christ into your own life, and painting another face with the colors of enmity and hatred.

—C.E. Macartney

213 At Home With Son's Killer

During the recent war a South Korean Christian, a civilian, was arrested by the communists and ordered shot. But when the young communist leader learned that the prisoner was in charge of an orphanage caring for small children, he decided to spare him and kill his son instead. So they shot the nineteen-year-old boy in the presence of his father.

Later the fortunes of war changed, and the young communist leader was captured by the United Nations forces, tried, and condemned to death. But before the sentence could be carried out, the Christian whose boy had been killed pleaded for the life of the killer. He declared that he was young, that he really did not know what he was doing. "Give him to me," said the father, "and I'll train him."

The United Nations forces granted the request, and that father took the murderer of his boy into his own home and cared for him. Today the young communist is a Christian pastor.

—T. Roland Philips

214 Epigram

●The Bible tells us to love our neighbours, and also to love our enemies; probably because they are generally the same people.

●Speak well of your enemies; remember you made them.

●You may have noticed that every enemy you made has ten friends. And every friend you made has ten more friends!

●The greatest conqueror is he who overcomes the enemy without a blow.

—Chinese Proverb

●"A Christian is not perfect; he is FORGIVEN."

—Seen on car's bumper stick

G

GIVING

215 Total Giving Statistics

Total religious contributions in 1976 are estimated at over $14 billion. That includes 9.5 billion from Protestants, 3.7 billion from Catholics, and 847 million from Jews.

The total given to all *charitable* causes in America came to about $26.88 billion.

216 Story Of A Dollar

A man put a note on a dollar bill and asked all who spent it to write down what it was spent for. In two weeks it was spent
>   five times for salary
>   five times for cigarettes
>   three times for candy
>   three times for meals
>   twice for clothes; twice for haircuts;
>   once for groceries; twice for laundry
>   once for car repairs; once for a magazine

But not once did it come to church!

217 Putting Saints Into Circulation

During the reign of Oliver Cromwell the government ran out of silver with which to make the coinage of the realm. Cromwell therefore sent his men everywhere to see if they could find more of the precious metal. They returned to report that the only silver they could find was in the statues of the saints which were on display in various cathedrals of the land. "Good!" replied Cromwell, "we will melt down the saints and put them into circulation!"

—H. G. Bosh

218 Hattie's 57 Pennies

Hattie Wiatt, a little girl, came to a small Sunday school and asked to be taken in, but it was explained there was no room for her. In less than two years she fell ill, and slipped away on her own little last pilgrimage and no one guessed her strange little secret until beneath her pillow was found a torn pocketbook with fifty-seven pennies in it, wrapped in a scrap of paper on which was written, "To help build the little Temple bigger, so that more children can go to Sunday school." For two years she had saved her pennies for the cause which was nearest her heart.

The pastor told the incident to his congregation, and the people began making donations for the enlargement. The papers told it far and wide, and within five years those fifty-seven pennies had grown to be $250,000, and today in Philadelphia, can be seen a great church, the Baptist Temple, seating 3,300, a Temple College with accommodations for more than 1,400 students, a Temple Hospital, and a Temple Sunday school so large that all who wish may come and be comfortable.

GIVING AND TITHING

219 Robbing God

Billy Graham, in his sermon "Partners with God," says: "One of the greatest sins in America today is the fact that we are robbing God of that which rightfully belongs to Him. When we don't tithe, we shirk a just debt. Actually we are not giving when we give God one-tenth, for it belongs to Him already. (Levt. 27:30). This is a debt we owe. Not until we have given a tenth do we actually *begin* making an offering to the Lord!"

220 Tithing Surprises

The Christian who tithe will be surprised:

(1) At the amount of money he has for the Lord's work
(2) At the deepening of his spiritual life in paying the tithe.
(3) At the ease in meeting his own obligation with the nine-tenths.
(4) At the ease in going from one-tenth to a larger percentage
(5) At the preparation this gives to be a faithful and wise steward over the nine-tenths remaining.
(6) At himself for not adopting the plan sooner!

221 Quaker Oats

Henry P. Crowell, affectionately called "The autocrat of the Breakfast Table," contracted tuberculosis when a boy and couldn't go to school. After hearing a sermon by Dwight L. Moody, young Crowell prayed, "I can't be a preacher, but I can be a good businessman. God, if You will let me make money, I will use it in Your service."

Under the doctor's advice Crowell worked outdoors for seven years and regained his health. He then bought the little run-down Quaker Mill at Ravanna, Ohio. Within ten years Quaker Oats was a household word to millions. Crowell also operated the huge Perfection Stove Company.

For over forty years Henry P. Crowell faithfully gave 60 to 70 percent of his income to God's causes, having advanced from an initial 10%.

222 Rockefeller's Testimony

Yes, I tithe, and I would like to tell you how it all came about. I had to begin work as a small boy to help support my mother. My first wages amounted to $1.50 per week. The first week after I went to work, I took the $1.50 home to my mother and she held the money in her lap and explained to me that she would be happy if I would give a tenth of it to the Lord.

I did, and from that week until this day I have tithed every dollar God has entrusted to me. And I want to say, if I had not tithed the first dollar I made I would not have tithed the first million dollars I made. Tell your readers to train the children to tithe, and they will grow up to be faithful stewards of the Lord.

—John D. Rockefeller, Sr.

223 The Colgate Story

A lad of 16 years named William left home to seek his fortune, all his possessions tied in a bundle carried in his hand. He met an old canal-boat captain. William told him his father was too poor to keep him and the only trade he knew was soap and candle making.

The old man then kneeled and prayed earnestly for the boy and advised: "Someone will soon be the leading soap-maker in New York. It can be you as well as someone else. Be a good man, give your heart to Christ, pay the Lord all that belongs to Him, make an honest soap; give a full pound, and I'm certain you'll be a prosperous and rich man."

Into the city, he remembered the captain's words, and though poor and lonesome, he united with a church. The first dollar earned, he gave 1/10 to God. Ten cents of every dollar were sacred to the Lord. Having regular employment, he soon became a partner and later sole owner of the business. He made an honest soap, gave a full pound and instructed his bookkeeper to open an account with the Lord of 1/10 of all income. The business grew, so he gave 2/10, 3/10, 4/10, 5/10 and finally he gave all his income.

This is the story of William Colgate, who has given millions to the Lord's cause.

224 "Innkeeper" Dependent On God

As a teenager, Wallace Johnson was fired by a sawmill operator. Today, as founder of Holiday Inns, he is a multimillionaire and called "the innkeeper of America."

Johnson started his business empire in 1939 with a borrowed $250. Since then he has helped provide jobs for 110,000 people. He is known nationwide for his Christian activities and stewardship as a Baptist layman.

"I am totally dependent on God for help in everything I do," he declares. "Otherwise, I honestly believe it would start to fall apart in months."

225 Senior Partner At Kraft

Years ago a young man began a small cheese business in Chicago. He failed. He was deeply in debt. "You didn't take God into your business. You have not worked with Him," said a Christian friend to him. Then the young man thought, "If God wants to run the cheese business, He can do it, and I'll work for Him and with Him!" From that moment, God became the senior partner in his business. The business grew and prospered and became the largest cheese concern in the world! You ask the name of that young man? J.L. Kraft who became president of the Kraft Cheese Company!

—Walter B. Knight

226 Story Of Welch Grape Juice

A young man accepted for the African missionary field reported at New York for "passage," but found on further examination that his wife could not stand the climate. He was heartbroken, but he prayerfully returned to his home and determined to make all the money he could to be used in spreading the Kingdom of God over the world. His father, a dentist, had started to make, on the side, an unfermented wine for the communion service. The young man took the business over and developed it until it assumed vast proportions—his name was "Welch," whose family still manufactures "grapejuice." He has given literally hundreds of thousands of dollars to the work of missions.

—The Presbyterian Advance

GOD, EXISTENCE OF

227 It Takes No Brains

Dwight D. Eisenhower said, "It takes no brains to be an atheist. Any stupid person can deny the existence of a supernatural power because man's physical senses cannot detect it. But there cannot be ignored the mystery of first life ... or the marvellous order in which the universe moves about us. All of these evidence the handiwork of a beneficent

Deity. For my part, that Deity is the God of the Bible and Christ, His Son."

228 Statistical Monstrosity

Said George Gallup, world-famed statistician, "I could prove God statistically! Take the human body alone. The chance that all the functions of the individual would just happen is a statistical monstrosity!"

229 God Is Sued

George Albrecht, 35, an electrician, filed a $25,000 damage suit against "God and Company," listing around 30 houses of worship and their clergymen as co-defendants, after he had lost an earlier damage suit against the city and a construction company. Albrecht had sought damages in the early suit for injuries received when a sidewalk collapsed under him during a rainstorm at a construction site. The trial jury ruled the accident as "an act of God," hence the second suit.

—*Christian Victory*

GOD, LOVE OF

230 The Fifth Sparrow

A little Spanish boy in Vigo who became a devout Christian was asked by an Englishman what had been the influence under which he acted. "It was all because of the odd sparrow," the boy replied. "I do not understand," said the Englishman in surprise. "What odd sparrow?"

"Well, Senor, it is this way," the boy said. "A gentleman gave me a Testament, and I read in one Gospel that two sparrows were sold for a farthing. And again in Luke, I saw, 'Are not five sparrows sold for two farthings...?' And I said to myself that Nuestro Senor ('our Lord') Jesus Christ knew well our custom of sell-

ing birds. As you know, Sir, we trap birds, and get one chico for two but for two chicos we throw in an extra sparrow. That extra sparrow is only a make-weight, and of no account at all.

"Now, I think to myself that I am so insignificant, so poor and so small that no one would think of counting me. I'm like the fifth sparrow. And yet, oh marvelous, Nuestro Senor says, 'Not one of them is forgotten before God.' I have never heard anything like it, Sir. No one but He could ever have thought of not forgetting me."

—King's Business

231 This Is How God Loves

In St. Paul's Cathedral, London is a life-size, marble statue of Christ writhing in anguish on the cross. The statue is subscribed: "This is how God loved the world!"

232 Love In 3 Dimensions

The Breadth: "God so loved the world"
The Length: "that He gave His only begotten Son"
The Depth: "that whosoever believeth on Him shall not perish"
The Height: But shall have everlasting Life."

GOD, OMNIPOTENCE

233 Hanging Upon Nothing

Martin Luther wrote to the prime minister in Germany: "I have lately seen a miracle. I looked out of the window at the stars in God's whole heavenly dome. I nowhere saw any pillars where the Master had placed such a dome still stands fast. There are some who seek such pillars and would like very much to feel and grasp them; because they cannot do it, they tremble and write as if the heavens would certainly fall for no other reason than that they cannot seize pillars. I would sooner expect to see the heavens fall than to see one jot or tittle of all the Word of God fail."

— *The Bible Friend*

GOD, PROMISES

235　Moody's Favorite Verse

Turning over a volume of valuable autographs, I came across the bold, manly signature of my old friend of many years, Dwight L. Moody. Underneath was his favourite text, which he calls up in an emergency. The text was Isaiah 1:7: "For the Lord God will help me. Therefore shall I not be confounded; therefore have I set my face like a flint; and I know that I shall not be ashamed."

— Walter Baxendale

234　Matter Into Energy

In northern Alabama some of our electricity comes from the Brown's Ferry nuclear plant near Decatur, Alabama. This is the world's largest nuclear energy plant. Its fuel is uranium. When just one gram of Uranium 235 fissions, it creates energy equivalent to 20 tons of TNT. One gram is about what a small birthday candle weighs. The candle, if burned, could hardly warm a cup of coffee.

This little one-gram candle, however, if converted 100% into energy, according to Einstein's equation, could produce the energy of 20,000 tons of TNT or 26.6 million kilowatt hours of electricity. What makes the difference between a one gram birthday candle that could hardly warm a cup of coffee and the same one gram candle that could provide the energy of 20,000 tons of TNT?

Einstein's equation is E equals MC^2. The E represents energy in ergs, mass grams and the C^2 is the velocity of the light squared. If we leave out the C^2 we get one erg is equal to one gram. One erg is less that the energy required for a mosquito to become airborne. If we add the C^2 we get 9×10^{20} centimeters per second. Thus we get one gram times 900,000,000,-000,000,000,000 (nine hundred quintillion) centimeters per second, equals 900,000,-000,000,000,000,000 ergs of energy.

This one gram candle, then, if transformed totally to energy is equivalent to the enormous power that a city of 40,000 people would use in one day. All of this when one gram of matter is changed into energy! God's creation pulsates with His might.

— *The Bible Friend*

236　Lifetime Rail Pass Goes Unused

We learned that when Crowfoot, the great chief of the Blackfoot confederacy in southern Alberta, gave the Canadian Pacific Railway permission to cross the Blackfoot land from Medicine Hat to Calgary, he was given in return a lifetime pass. Crowfoot put it in a leather case and carried it around his neck for the rest of his life. There is no record, however, that he availed himself of the right to travel anywhere on the CPR trains.

God's promises are not for decoration.

— *Prairie Overcomer*

237　Epigram

●I believe the promises of God enough to venture an eternity on them.

— G. Campbell Morgan

●If I could hear Christ praying for me in the next room, I would not fear a million enemies. Yet distance makes no difference. He is praying for me: "He ever liveth to make intercession."

— Robert Murray McCheyne

GOSSIPING

238 "G" For Gossip

R. G. LeTourneau, was for many years an outstanding Christian businessman — heading a company which manufactured large earthmoving equipment. He once remarked, "We used to make a scraper known as 'Model G.' One day somebody asked our salesman what the 'G' stood for. The man, who was pretty quick on the trigger, immediately replied, I'll tell you. The "G" stands for gossip because like a talebearer this machine moves a lot of dirt and movest it fast!"

239 Luther Never Divulged Confession

Even though he had been a priest for twenty eight years. Martin Luther, who fell away from the priesthood and the Catholic faith, never revealed anything he had heard in confession.

He left the Church, married a nun, preached and wrote against the Catholic Church and everyone and everything in it. but he never told a single thing he had heard in confession.

— Arthur Tonne

240 Six Articles Of Wesley's Covenant

In 1752 a group of men, including John Wesley, who were nicknamed Methodist, signed a covenant which every man might hang on his study wall. The six articles of the solemn agreement follow:

1. That we will not listen or willingly inquire after ill concerning one another;

2. That, if we do hear any ill of each other, we will not be forward to believe it;

3. That as soon as possible we will communicate what we hear by speaking or writing to the person concerned;

4. That until we have done this, we will not write or speak a syllable of it to any other person;

5. That neither will we mention it, after we have done this, to any other person;

6. That we will not make any exception to any of these rules unless we think ourselves absolutely obliged in conference.

— Evangelistic Illustration

H

HATRED

241 The Spite House

Joseph Richardson, a New York millionaire lived and died in a house only five feet wide. It was called the "Spite House," and it deserved its name. Owning the narrow lot of land on which it was built, Mr. Richardson wished to sell it to the neighboring property owners. They would not pay him what he asked, and so he put up this house, which disfigured the block—and then condemned himself to a life of discomfort in it.

—Golden Rule

242 The Devil's Lane

Two of our neighbors had a falling-out over the boundary line fence between their farms. Feelings became so intense that each built his own fence. These fences were built about four feet apart. Not only were they added expenses, but neither of the neighbors had the use of the four-foot strip of land—it rightfully belonged to neither of them. For lack of a better name, this four-foot strip was called "The Devil's Lane." I guess it was rightly named because Old Bellzebub did take control of it. At least he controlled the men involved.

—Carl C. Williams

HEAVEN

243 Car Sickness All Forgotten

A visiting pastor spoke at the Winona Lake Brethren Church. He told the congregation that as a child he used to have a terrible time with car sickness. He would travel for 20 miles and throw up. He soon developed an inferiority complex from his childhood because his parents would apologize for him whenever they ride with someone else.

It so happened that his grandma lived 100 miles from home, and the trips to grandma's were always terrible. But once arrived, he would take off his shoes and roam around the beautiful country. Grandma would bake the most delicious cake and always say "yes." For two to three years, he would thoroughly enjoy his stay at grandma's, until it was time to return.

And while at grandma's, the preacher

concluded. he had forgotten all about the car-sick trip going there. "God shall wipe away all tears from their eyes ... for the former things are passed away" (Rev. ¹:4).

244 Just Think
Of stepping on shore.
    And finding it heaven:
Of taking hold of a hand.
    And finding it God's hand:
Of breathing new air.
    And finding it heavenly air:
Of feeling invigorated.
    And finding it immortality:
Of passing from storm and
    Tempest to an unbroken calm:
Of waking up—
    And finding it HOME!
                        —Selected

245 No Other Song But Christ
The beloved hymn "Over the Sunset Mountains" was penned during the writer's meditation on the piano. Sure that its message would catch on, Peterson confidently approached a publisher.

"We would like to use it," the approving publisher said after glancing over it, "but we have one little suggestion. Can you take out his reference to Jesus and enlarge a little more on heaven?"

Heaven without Jesus? Unthinkable! Clutching his manuscript. the composer walked from the publisher's office with another song coming on: "I Have No Song to Sing, but that of Christ, my King." Both songs have become favorites with Christians.

246 An Advertisement Of Heaven
Here is an ad from the Bible:
FREE
BEAUTIFUL HOMES
to be

GIVEN AWAY
in a
PERFECT CITY!
with:
100% Pure Water Free
No Light Bills
Perpetual Lighting
Permanent Pavement
Nothing Undersirable
Everything New
Perfect Health
Immunity from Accidents
The Best of Society
Beautiful Music
Free Transportation
SECURE A CONTRACT TODAY FOR THE NEW JERUSALEM.
                        —The Bible Friend

247 Indestructible Sky
Mr. Einstein. the great scientist was strolling along the Princeton Promenade one beautiful starlit night. Looking up into the sky. and sighing wearily. he said. "Anyway. that the atom cannot destroy."

HELL

248 Hell Is
A Place of Consciousness (Luke 16:23,24)
A Place of Torment (Luke 16:23,24,28)
A Place of Darkness (Matthew 8:12)
Eternal Separation from loved ones who are believers (Luke 13:28)
Without the Slightest Hope of Release (Matthew 25:46, Hebrews 6:2)
The Torment of Memory in Hell (Luke 16:27,28)

249 Trends On Hell
A Gallup Poll showed most Europeans believe in heaven but not in hell. In Sweden. the least orthodox nation, only 60 percent believed in God.

250 No Way To Describe Hell

There is no way to describe Hell. Nothing on earth can compare with it. No living person has any real idea of it. No madman in wildest flights of insanity ever beheld its horror. No man in delirium ever picture a place so utterly terrible as this. No nightmare racing across a fevered mind ever produces a terror to match that of the mildest hell.

No murder scene with splashed blood and oozing wound ever suggested a revulsion that could touch the border lands of hell. Let the most gifted writer exhaust his skill in describing this roaring caverns of unending flame, and he would not even brushed in fancy the nearest edge of hell.

Hell was originally "prepared for the Devil and his angels"—not for man! Little wonder that there is joy in heaven over one sinner that repented. He is saved, redeemed, rescued. It makes the hearts in heaven glad.

—Selected

251 Archibald Boyle Of "Hell Club"

Archibald Boyle was a resident of Glasgow, and the leading member of a wicked and infidel association called "The Hell Club." The efforts of its members were to outdo each other in blasphemy and debauchery. At their meeting, Boyle, by his culture, boldness, and brilliant talents, outshone all; while, outside of the club, he was a favorite in female society.

One night, after returning from his carousals in the club, he dreamed, that as he was riding home on his black horse, in the darkness, someone seized the reins, and said, "You must go with me!" "And who are you?" cried Boyle, struggling to free the reins from the intruder's grasp. "That you will see by and by," was the cold reply.

Boyle spurred his horse cruelly; and the steed flew forward with a speed that nearly deprived his rider of breath. The mysterious guide still kept his hold of the reins. Boyle made one more desperate effort to disengage his reins from the iron grasp of his guide. His horse reared and plunged; Boyle was thrown, and fell down, down, down, with ever-increasing velocity.

Discovering his resistless attendant at his side, he exclaimed, "Where are you taking me? Where am I? Where am I going?" "To hell," replied the unrelenting voice. They hurried forward till the echoes of the groans and yells of frantic revelry saluted their ears. They entered a grand arched way, and stood within the precincts of hell. There Boyle beheld the inmates, chasing the same phantoms they had pursued in life.

He soon perceived that he was surrounded by those whom he had known on earth, and ventured to address his former friend Mrs. D., who he saw sitting, as she was wont on earth, apparently absorbed in her favorite game of loo. "Ha, Mrs. D.! delighted to see you: d'ye know a fellow told me to-night he was bringing me to hell? Ha, ha! if this be hell, what a devilish pleasant place it must be! Ha, ha! Come now, Mrs. D., for auld lang syne, do just stop for a moment, rest, and," he was about to add, "show me through the pleasures of hell;" when she answered, with a shriek that awoke awful echoes as loud as thunder, "THERE IS NO REST IN HELL!"

The lady unclasped the vest of her gorgeous robe, and displayed to his shuddering gaze a coil of living snakes writhing, stinging, darting, in her bosom. Others followed her example. In some, he saw throbbing hearts, on which distilled drops of molten metal, under which they writhed in hopeless agony. In every bosom, he saw that which we cannot conceive or describe, so horrible was the vision. They laughed and sang and blasphemed, as they had done on earth.

Then he heard an unearthly voice proclaim, "These are the pleasures of hell," which echoed mockingly like distant thunder. He saw those who had the sinful pleasures they loved in life. He saw a companion of his boyish profligacy rushing on, as if in the heat of the chase, and called to him. Scarcely had he uttered the words, before the wild yell of ten thousand voices stunned his terror-stricken ear, "There is no rest in hell."

Boyle tried to shut his eyes, but could not: he tried to rest upon the pavement, but was by it instantly thrown upon his feet. He was compelled to gaze upon the steady torrent of woe and horror. His conductor stood again by his side. Boyle addressed him, "Take me from this place! by the living God, whose name I have so often outraged, I adjure thee, take me from this place!"—"Canst thou still name his name?" replied his guide, "Go then; but, in a year and a day, we meet to part no more."

At this, Boyle awoke, feeling that these last words were as letters of fire burned into his very heart. He was unable to leave his bed for several days. The impression was so deep, that he resolved never again to attend the club. His old companions flocked around him, and used every artifice to draw him back to his old ways. At last, one of them won upon his confidence by feigning similar disgust with his former life. To him, Boyle related his dream. The decoy then turned upon him with great power of ridicule, and gained his purpose.

At the club, again he found no relief. He grew haggard and gray under the lash of conscience and fear of the future. He shrank from the annual meeting, when the time allotted him by his guide in his dream would expire; but his companions **forced him to attend.** Every nerve of his body writhed in agony at the first sentence of the president's opening address: "Gentlemen, this is leap year; therefore it is a year and a day since our last annual meeting."

Boyle would have rushed from the room, had he dared. He could bear the wrath of the Almighty easier than the sneers of his fellows. They plied him with wine; but his wit was gloomy, and his laugh fiendish. At the close, he mounted his horse to ride home.

In the morning, his horse was discovered grazing quietly by the roadside, and a few yards distant lay the stiffened corpse of Archibald Boyle. The dream was fulfilled. The strange guide claimed him at the appointed time.

—Selected

HOLY SPIRIT

252 Moody's Experience

One day in New York—what a day! I can't describe it! I seldom refer to it! It is almost too sacred to name! I can only say God revealed Himself to me! I had such an experience of love that I had to ask Him to stay His hand! I went to preaching again. The sermons were no different. I did not present any new truth. Yet hundreds were converted. I would not be back where I was before that blessed experience if you would give me Glasgow!

—Dwight L. Moody

253 Fill Us!

"This the secret of the holy,
Not our holiness, but HIM:
Jesus! empty us and fill us
With Thy fulness to the brim."

254 Filling Is Answer

Paul tells us to live victoriously and to avoid excesses of the flesh. Moody once illustrated this truth as follows: "Tell me," he said to his audience. "How can I get the air out of this glass?" One man said, "Suck it out with a pump." Moody replied, "That would create a vacuum and shatter the glass." After many impossible suggestions, Moody smiled, picked up a pitcher of water, and filled the glass. "There," he said, "all the air is now removed." He then went on to show that victory in the Christian life is not by "sucking out a sin here and there," but rather by being filled with the Spirit.

—Mrs. Ruby Miller

HONESTY

255 Down Trend In U.S.

In 1924 *Liberty* magazine sent out 100 letters to people selected at random throughout the U.S., enclosing $1 bill, saying it was an adjustment of an error which the addressed had complained of — which really did not exist. Of the 100 recipients, 27 returned the dollar, saying it was a mistake.

Then in 1971, *Liberty* again conducted the same test. But now only 13 returned the money!

256 Shortchanging: Billion-Dollar Business

Bilking consumers out of pennies has now become a billion-dollar business. The *National Observer* noted that short weighing on food, gasoline, home fuel oil, packaged hardware items, and pills cost the American public some six to twelve billion dollars per year. In an effort to curb this swindle, whether accidental or intentional, many states are spot-checking weighs and measures.

Pennsylvania investigators discovered that 15.5 percent of all prepackaged foods checked were short weighted, with some stores shorting on 25 percent of the packages checked. A three-day Kansas investigation turned up evidence that 30 percent of all meat packaged in eleven stores were short weighted.

In Arkansas, officials checked one pound cans of vegetables to find none that contained sixteen ounces. And Tennessee officials found prepackaged pork chops short weighted by up to thirty-one cents. Officials have tabulated forty-eight ways to cheat in weighing meat in from of customers, and many markets are apparently using some of them.

—C.R. Hembree

257 Honor System For Tolls Failed

During the summer of 1970, the state of Delaware experimented with the honor system for twenty days on the Delaware Turnpike. Motorists without exact change at the automatic toll booth were allowed to take appropriately addressed envelopes and mail in the money.

But in twenty days, of more than 26,000 envelopes taken, only 582 were returned, according to the *Associated Press*. And of those that were returned, some contained stamps and pieces of paper instead of money. The experiment cost the state about $4,000 before it was discontinued. And that didn't include lost tolls.

258 Ready-To-Go Term Papers

Sunday, 8:15 p.m. A junior at the University of Miami walks into the dingy third-floor office of "Universal International Termpapers Limited, Inc." He scribbles out his order and hands it to the clerk. "I'm sorry," she says, "We don't have that paper in stock. We'll have to order it." The clerk dials the firm's main office in Boston and then attaches the telephone receiver to a copying machine. A few minutes later, page after page of an impressively researched paper, transm ted from Boston, rolls off the copier.

—Tin

HUSBAND AND WIFE

259 Paying Wife $3.40 Per Hour

At the annual meeting of the Vanier Institute of the Family held in Winnipeg, proposals were outlined which would provide the homemaker with a salary. Dr. David Ross of the Canadian Council on Social Development said during a panel discussion that a "dad-to-mom" type of transfer is feasible if taxpayers are willing to forgo personnel exemptions. Dr. Ross proposed paying housewives one of three salaries: $100 a month, $1.90 an hour, or $3.40 an hour.

The $100 a month salary—which would cost the federal government $2.6 billion in lost taxes—would be financed without a tax increase if all personal exemptions were eliminated, Dr. Ross said.

—*Prairie Overcomer*

260 Who Is Worth More?

Economists from the Chase Manhattan Bank have attempted to settle the argument about who is worth more around the house, the husband or the wife.

The economists estimate that the typical American housewife spends 99.6 hours each week in work around the house. Labor value is based on the going rate for services performed.

The bank concludes that a wife is worth $159.34 per week or $8,285.68 a year. This is what it would cost the husband to hire special workers to perform the services to the home.

The American husband's wages in house work, if paid, would total only $51.01 per week, less than one third the wages of his wife. This is for such duties as garbage man, lawn mower, night watchman, accountant, fashion consultant, youth counselor, etc.

261 Giving Her Right Hand

During the Crusades, a knight was taken captive by the Moslem Saladin. The knight begged for his life, claiming that he had a wife in England who loved him dearly. Saladin commented that she would soon forget him and marry another. On second thought, the cruel chieftain offered to set the man free if the lady in question would send her right hand as token of her love for this captive.

When word was sent to this lady in England, she immediately cut off her right hand and sent it to Saladin. The man was forthwith returned to England.

There is a statue of this faithful woman in one of the old cathedrals of England. She is attractive, but the statue shows her without the right hand.

262 The Word "Sweetheart"

Margaret was the widow of the powerful Scot Baliol of Norway. She carried her husband's embalmed heart in an ivory box for twenty-one years, calling it her "sweet heart and silent companion."

When dying, she asked "that the heart be laid upon her breast, so that two hearts united may spend all eternity together." This inspired the first usage of the term "sweetheart."

HYPOCRISY

263 The Two-Faced Butler

A very odd bit of sculpture adorns the wall on the grounds of Ribston Hall, Yorkshire, England. It is what is commonly called "The Two-faced Butler." On one side there is a face that is all smiles and politeness; on the other side is one that depicts nothing but insolence and impoliteness.

It is told that this represents just such a butler who once served the household. One day after having received orders from the mistress of the household, all smiles and obsequiousness, he was seen a moment later when he thought she was not looking, sticking out his tongue at her and making other impolite gestures. So this statue was ordered made and erected in a very prominent spot to both shame him and warn any other servants who might have a tendency to imitate the behavior of the two-faced butler.

—*Evangelistic Illustration*

264 Rajah's Double Life

Shahaji Bavasahib, Maharajah of the native State of Kolhapur, India, was a proud Indian potentate in the daytime and a highway robber at night. Kolhapur is situated within the Dekkan division of Bombay and has an area of 3,217 square miles with a population of about a million. The exalted autocrat would don the disguise of a bandit each night and lead a murderous masked gang against his own subjects, plundering and looting their possessions. At intervals he would raid his own state treasury and purloin its contents as well as the crown jewels. The latter would invariably turn up in distant pawnshops where the government would periodically redeem them at state expense. The maharajah would cap his hypocrisy by issuing mandates against the looters and offering a prize for their capture.

—Robert Ripley

265 Some Hymns We Really Sing

(1) "When morning gilds the skies / My heart awaking cries / Oh no, another day"
(2) Amazing grace, how sweet the sound / that saved a wretch like you."
(3) Jesus, I am resting, resting / Resting, resting, resting, rest.
(4) The strife is o'er, the battle done / Our church has split and our side won.
(5) The church's one foundation / Is Tax-deductible.
(6) My hope is built on nothing.

I

INTEGRITY

266 Lawmaker's Code Of Ethics

On March 2, 1977, the House of Representative approved by 402-22 vote a Code of Ethics for its members. It contained a strong financial requirement (gifts totalling $100 in one year from a single source) and set a limit on outside earnings (15% of a member's current salary or $8,625).

267 Rather Be Right Than President

Famous men of the past have bequeathed us statement that have become mottoes. History declares that Henry Clay was about to introduce a certain bill in Congress when a friend said, "If you do, Clay, it will kill your chance for the presidency."

"But is the measure right?" Clay asked, and on being assured it was right said, "I would rather be right than be president."

— *The Watchman Examiner*

268 Let Illinois Be Honest!

In one of his books Samuel Smiles tells of the terrible temptation that once came to the state of Illinois. America was passing through great financial depression. Governments were faced with financial panic. The rich state of Pennsylvania set the example of repudiating its debts. Illinois, then a poor state, felt that with such a lead it was justified in following suit.

When Stephen Douglas heard it, he resolved, though very ill, to oppose it with all his might. He was carried to his place in the legislature on a stretcher. Lying on his back he moved the historic resolution: "That Illinois be honest." The motion touched the deepest sentiment of every member. It was adopted with enthusiasm. It dealt a deathblow to the system of repudiation. And Illinois became one of the most prosperous states of America.

— J. A. Clark

269 Epigram

● Few men have virtue to withstand the highest bidder.

— George Washington

● I would rather fail in a cause that someday will triumph than to win in a cause that I know someday will fail.

— Woodrow Wilson

● Character is a victory, not a gift.

● A precious stone; though it falls into the mire, does not thereby lose its brilliance.
—Malay Proverbs

● The measure of a man's real character is what he would do, if he knew he would never be found out.
—Macaulay

● Two opposing candidates were debating on a street corner while a group of spectators listened. "There are hundreds of ways of making money," challenged one, "but only one honest way."

"And what's that?" jeered the other.

"Aha!" exulted the first speaker. "I knew you wouldn't know."
—Capper's Weekly

ISRAEL, BIRTH OF

270 Babylonian? Hittite?

Have you ever met a Babylonian? Or a Hittite or an Assyrian or a Philistine or an Amalekite? At one time these were great nations. Today, they are extinct.

The Jews exist today as a modern, independently recognized people with their own state in Palestine.

271 Israel Is Born!

The British High Commissioner for Palestine departed May 14, 1948, and —on the same day—the Jewish National Council and the General Zionist Council, meeting in Tel Aviv, proclaimed the establishment of a Jewish State to be called Israel.

Mr. David Ben Gurion was appointed Prime Minister, and Dr. Chaim Wiezmann elected President of the Provisional Council.

272 Significant Year: 1948

The year 1948 appears to have been a significant turning point in hastening the events of the last days.

In that year the *State of Israel* officially came into existence, a most significant event in the light of Biblical prophecy.

The *National Council of Churches* was organized in 1948. This world religious body, obsessed with ecumenicity at the expense of doctrine, has contributed significantly toward today's widespread apostasy.

In 1948 *missionaries were being barred from* the China mainland by revolutionary forces, which finally took over the government of China in 1949. Result: One-fourth of the world's population barred from feeding upon God's word.

The beginnings of *the Common Market* occurred in 1948 when the Hague Congress initiated a Council of Europe which included a Consultive Assembly (Parliament), a Committee of Ministers and a permanent secretariat. In 1948 Belgium, the Netherlands and Luxumberg also established a Benelux customs union among themselves.

In 1948 communists over-run Czechoslovakia and blockaded Berlin. These two events triggered formation of the *North Atlantic Treaty Organization* (NATO), perhaps the only deterrent to Russian's taking over Western Europe. That same year saw also the formation of the *Organization of American States* (OAS).

The *space age began in 1948*. In that year experiments with liquid hydrogen proved that a rocket could be sent beyond earth's gravitational pull.
—*Moody Monthly*

ISRAEL-REGATHERING

273 Pattern Of Immigration

Here is a statistical summary showing the pattern of Jewish immigration back to the land of Palestine:

First, there had been no Jew in the city of Jerusalem, and only a handful in the entire land of Palestine. By the year 1880, about 25,000 had by one way or another got into the land. By 1914, at the beginning of World War I, we see *90,000* Jews in Palestine. By 1923, there were *180,000.* By 1935, *300,000.* By 1937, *430,000.* By 1945, *500,000.* And when independence came in 1948, there were *650,000.*

After independence, immigration became a flood. The first immigrants to come en masse were *25,000* survivors of the Nazi holocaust. Altogether, *33,000* arrived during the first four months of the State. The new state's first year's total immigrants numbered *204,000.* And before three more years passed, an additional *655,000* had entered.

Thus, by the end of 1965, total Israeli population was *2.2 million.* By 1969, it was *2.8 million.* By 1970, *3 million.* By 1976, *3.5 million.* Of this population today, one half are now Israel-born, one-fourth are of European origin, and one-fourth of Afro-Asian origin.

274 From All Directions

As soon as the State of Israel was proclaimed in 1948, they came from the "four corners of the earth"—north, east, south and west.

"I will say to the north, Give up" (Isaiah 43:5-6)—The Jews came into Palestine from every nation in Europe. Czechoslovakia permitted 20,000 of its surviving Jews to depart. About 30,000 came from Turkey, 36,000 from Bulgaria. More than half of the Jews in Yugoslavia returned.

"I will bring thy seed from the east"— Prior to independence, 87% of the Jews who returned to Palestine came from European countries, with only 10% from Oriental countries. During the first year and a half of Israel's independence, there was an increase of 37% of Jews from the Orient, and by 1953 the percentage had reached 50%. Eight hundred Jews came from Shanghai and Hongkong.

"I will say to the south, Keep not back"—Jews were living in most of the Arab lands even before the advent of the

Arabs. In Libya, there was a prosperous Jewish community six hundred years before the Arab conquest there. About 900,000 Jews dwelt in Arab lands before the establishment of Israel. Today, there are only about 40,000 Jews in the Arab world. They have returned to Israel.

"I will gather thee from the west"— There was a virtual stampede from Egypt, Morocco, Tunis, Algeria, Europe, the United States and most of the Latin American countries.

275 Law Of Return

In 1950 the Knesset (Parliament) of Israel enacted the Law of Return which guaranteed the right of every Jew to immigrate to the homeland.

Harry Golden wrote in *Holiday:* "The minimum requirement to immigrate into Israel is the statement, 'I am a Jew,' The immigrant needs no papers, no testimonials, no affidavits signed by rabbis, no religious tests. Here for the first time, immigrants may come into a country where they are not punctured by needles or forced to display their teeth."

ISRAEL-TEMPLE

276 A Fervent Prayer

The daily prayer of faithful Jews all over the world had been, "May it be acceptable to Thee, Eternal God, our God and the God of our fathers, that the sanctuary may be rebuilt speedily in our days and our portion assigned us in Thy law. There will we serve Thee in reverence as of old in bygone days."

And in 1967—for the first time in 1897 years—the Jews took control of the temple area.

277 Training School For Priests

Meanwhile, a special school has been established in Israel to train young Israelis of the tribe of Levi in ancient rites of sacrifice. Called "Yeshiva Avodas Hakodesh," the school was founded by Rabbi Hirsh Ha-Cohen and dedicated in December, 1970. Only students who could trace their ancestry to Aaron are admitted. There they learn the laws of ancient animal sacrifice and how to perform the practices which existed in the ancient Temple.

278　Original Temple Furnishing May Be Found

It may be that they will even relocate the original furnishings of the holy place and the holy of holies, for history never recorded their destruction. In fact, there is strong tradition to indicate that they are still in existence, ready to be revealed in the end time when they will be used again.

Perhaps the furnishings of the holy place are in Rome where they were taken after the Roman conquests of Judea. Though later captured by the Vandals in A.D. 544, the Temple Menorah, the table for shewbread, the garments of the priest, along with the silver trumpets which were sounded for morning and evening sacrifice, may have ended up in Constantinople when the Vandal Kingdom was overthrown.

Even though the vessels of the first temple were taken to Babylon (cf. Jer. 28:3), perhaps the ark of the covenant is hidden out on Mount Nebo where the book of 2 Maccabees (2:1-7) says that the prophet Jeremiah hid it. Or it may be hidden under the temple area, somewhere in the vast recesses of Solomon's quarries which run under the city, where another tradition says that the ark was hidden.

—Walter K. Price

J

JESUS CHRIST

279 Plowed Into History

Ralph Waldo Emerson has said, "The name of Jesus is not so much written as plowed into the history of the world." And men never tire of reading about Him.

280 I Am So Glad

I am so glad He was not born
    In some rich palace bed.
I am so glad to know it was
    A lowly place, instead,
A place where soft-eyed cows and sheep
    Were sheltered and were fed.
For to the country-born of earth
    A stable will ever be
A wholesome place, where night comes down
    With its tranquillity,
A place of heart's ease and content
    For all who choose to see.

And so I like to think of Him,
    First opening His eyes
In that good elemental place
    Beneath the friendly skies,
That the men of fields could find Him there,

As well as the great and wise.
    —Grace Noll Crowell

282 "What A Night"

That night when in the Judean skies
The mystic star dispensed its light,
A blind man moved in his sleep
And dreamed that he had sight.

That night when shepherds heard
The song of hosts angelic choiring near,
A deaf man stirred in slumber's spell
And dreamed that he could hear.

That night when o'er the new-born babe
The tender Mary rose to lean,
A loathsome leper smiled in sleep,
And dreamed that he was clean.

That night when in the manger lay
The Sanctified who came to save,
A man moved in the sleep of death,
And dreamed there was no grave.
    —Selected

281 Why Was He Silent?

Why is He silent when a word,
    Would slay His accusers all?
Why does He meekly bear their taunts,

86

When angels wait His call?
"He was made sin," my sin He bore
Upon the accursed tree,
And sin hath no defense to make,
His silence was for me!

283 "Christ the Consoler"

Tissot, the artist, following the fashion of the day, was spending his talent in painting the society women of Paris. In his time it was quite the thing for wealthy and pleasure-loving women to sing in the choir of some large church that they might appear to be religious-minded.

Tissot planned to paint a picture with the title, "The Choir Singer." He went to the great Church of St. Sulpice in Paris to study the setting for his picture. Into his soul came a vision altogether different from what he was planning at the time.

He seemed to see the ruins of a large castle with windows and walls broken and shattered. In the debris sat a weary peasant and his wife, with a small bundle, their only earthly belongings, resting beside them. They were a picture of despair. While they sat, the artist saw in vision a figure of a Man with bleeding hands and feet and a crown on His head. It was the Man of Sorrows. He sat beside the weeping pair, in order to console them. When the artist returned to his studio, he tried to continue on the canvas he had planned, but constantly there came before him the vision of Christ showing compassion to the old couple. He turned his talent to paint that scene and called it "Christ the Consoler."

—Selected

284 Three Crosses

Three crosses on a lonely hill,
A thief on either side,
And, in between, the Son of God ...
How wide the gulf - how wide!

Yet one thief spanned it with the words,
"Oh Lord, remember me";

The other scoffed and turned aside
To lost eternity.

Forsaken is the hilltop now,
And all the crosses gone,
But in believing hearts of men
The center cross lives on.

And still, as when these sentinels
First met earth's wondering view,
The presence of the Lord divides—
Upon which side are you?
—Helen Franzee Bower

285 Garden Tomb's Soil Analyzed

When the Garden Tomb was discovered in 1885, the godly General Gordon was convinced that this was the place where the body of Jesus had lain. There is a traditional tomb inside the wall of modern Jerusalem, but no certainty attaches to the site.

The Garden Tomb, hidden for centuries, was covered with rubbish twenty feet high. When they first cleared the spot, with great caution they gathered all the dust and debris within the tomb and carefully shipped it to the Scientific Association of Great Britain. Every part of it was analyzed, but there was no trace of human remains. If this is the real tomb of Christ, then Jesus was the first to be laid there and he was also the last.
—Alliance Weekly

286 The Jefferson Bible

In the 18th century, the U.S. Congress once issued a special edition of Thomas Jefferson's Bible. It was a simple copy of our Bible with all references to the supernatural eliminated. Jefferson, in selecting, had confined himself solely to the moral teachings of Jesus.

The closing words of this Bible are: "There laid they Jesus and rolled a great stone at the mouth of the sepulchere and departed."

Thank God, our Bible ended with the news that "He is risen!"

287   Easy To Invent Christianity?

During the French Revolution, somebody said to Talleyrand, bishop of Autun: "The Christian religion—what is it? It would be easy to start a religion like that."

"Oh, yes," Talleyrand replied. "One would only have to get crucified and rise again the third day."

—*Scrapbook*

288   Fragrance From Crown Of Thorns

An ancient legend tells of a monk who found the crown of thorns which had pressed on the Master. On Good Friday morning he set the crown on a side altar of the cathedral. It was a cruel looking, ghastly thing, covered with blood. The people glanced at it for a moment and then turned away. It reminded them too keenly of the ugliness and cruelty of their sins.

There the crown remained until Easter morning when, with the sunrise, the monk made his way into the sanctuary. He thought that this bloody reminder of Good Friday would be out of place, and he should remove it. As he approached the altar, he detected a strange fragrance. The sun was so bright he could not at first notice what had happened. The sun had centered its rays upon the crown, and had changed the sharp thorns and the cruel twigs into roses of the rarest beauty and the most pleasing fragrance.

—*Selected*

289   First Sunrise Service

The year was 1909. The place was Mount Roubidoux in California. In the valley at the foot of the mountain was Mission Inn. Here, staying as a guest, was Jacob Riis, the famous social crusader and father of slum clearance in New York.

As Riis looked up at the crest of Mount Roubidoux, he caught a vision. At the evening song service of the inn, he passed along his thoughts to Frank Miller, the inn proprietor, and the assembled guests:

"I see in the days to come an annual pilgrimage—call it what you will—winding its way up the steeps of Mount Roubidoux, climbing ever higher toward the cross that crowns the summit, where the dell peels out its message of peace on earth and good will to men, and gathering there to sing the old songs that go straight to the hearts of men and women."

Riis spoke as a true prophet, but even he could never have dreamed how soon his words would come true. The next Sunday was Easter, and Miller decided to make its observance memorable. He invited one hundred of his guests and friends—Riis had left by then—to climb with him at dawn to the summit of Mount Roubidoux and there to hail the breaking of the holy day with a simple, impressive service.

In the light of that Easter dawn of 1909, the first sunrise service on record was held by those one hundred pilgrims.

—*Franklin Winters*

JUDGING ANOTHER

290   Mutual Distrust Aboard Ship

The folly of snap judgments of others is well illustrated by a story the late Bishop Potter of New York used to tell on himself.

He was sailing for Europe in one of the great transatlantic liners. When he went on board, he found another passenger was to share the cabin with him. After going to see his accommodations, he came up to the purser's desk and inquired if he could leave his gold watch and other valuables in the ship's safe. He explained that ordinarily he never availed himself of that privilege, but he had been to his cabin and had met the man who was to occupy the other berth and, judging from his appearance, he was afraid that he might not be a trustworthy person.

The purser accepted the responsibility of caring for the valuables, and remarked; "It 's all right, Bishop, I'll be very glad to take care of them for you. The other man has been up here and left his for the same reason."

—H. A. Ironside

291 Walking In His Moccasins

Among the Sioux Indians there prevailed in the days of the frontier a strange custom. If one of the tribes determined to travel for a little while in areas guarded by other tribes, always on the night before he left his camp, the traveler would be required to sit with the chiefs of the Sioux tribe around a campfire and then before it fell back into gray ash he would be asked to arise and, silhouetted against the flames, would lift this prayer, "Great Spirit, help me to never judge another until I have walked two weeks in his moccasins."

—Joseph R. Sizoo

292 Quieting The Orphan Baby

Several years ago a Santa Fe train was speeding through Oklahoma. In one of the coaches sat a young woman desperately trying to take care of a restless baby, whose crying was evidently annoying some of the passengers.

Across the aisle sat a stout fellow, a picture of comfort and rich living. He glowered over at the woman and shouted: "Can't you keep that child quiet?" On taking a further look at the young lady, he noticed that her dress was one of mourning.

Then he heard her say gently: "I cannot help it. The child is not mine. I am doing my best."

"Where is its mother?" asked the portly passenger.

"In her coffin, sir," answered the young lady,"in the baggage car up ahead."

The steely eyes of the fat fellow filled with tears. He got up, took the babe in his arms, kissed it, and then walked up and down the aisle with the child, trying his best to soothe the motherless little one and make up for his harshness.

—Selected

293 Epigram

●Longfellow: "If we could only read the secret history of our enemies, we would find in each man's life, sorrow and suffering enough to disarm all hostility."

●Search seven times before you suspect anyone.

—Japanese Proverb

●Never judge a man by what he says; try and find out why he said it.

●When you meet a man, you judge him by his clothes; when you leave, you judge him by his heart.

—Russian Proverb

●Believe me, every man has his secret sorrows, which the world knows not; and oftentimes we call a man cold when he is only sad.

—Longfellow

●It is unfortunate that God didn't think to give us our neighbors' children, since these are the only ones we know.

—*Stuff and Nonsense*

●One should pity the blind, but it's hard to do if the rascal is the umpire.

●We judge ourselves by what we feel capable of doing, while others judge us by what we have already done.

—Longfellow

●Voice over the phone: I sent my little son, James, to your store for five pounds of apples, and I find on weighing them that you sent only four and a quarter pounds.

The Grocer: Madam, my scales are regularly inspected and are correct. Have you weighed your little boy?

KINDNESS

294 "You Called Me Brother"

Tolstoy, the great Russian writer, was passing along a street one day when a begger stopped him and pleaded for alms. The great Russian searched through his pockets for a coin, but finding none he regretfully said, "Please don't be angry with me, my brother, but I have nothing with me. If I did I would gladly give it to you."

The beggar's face flamed up, and he said, "You have given me more than I asked for. You have called me brother."

—Evangelistic Illustration

295 Beethoven's "Moonlight Sonata"

Who has not been thrilled by Beethoven's "Moonlight Sonata?" It is a master interpretation in sound of the unspeakable glory of a moonlight night. This beautiful piece of music was created because the composer wanted to give something of himself and his talent to a blind girl.

This lady could not see the beauties of a moonlight night: blind was she to the silver sheen on trees and shrub and grass; blind was she to the silver covering on the lake; blind was she to the world of milky white in the sky. So the thoughtful and selfless Beethoven put his genius to work. He would tell her not merely in words, but in sound, of the beauty her eyes could not behold.

As a result the world has been enriched. He gave the best of his talent in a selfless act of kindness.

—Tonne

296 The Janitor's Guest

Years ago a Missouri country congregation listened to a sermon by a young preacher who had walked twenty miles to deliver it. Tired, hungry, this youth faltered, floundered, and failed. The people were disgusted; they did not know he had walked the weary miles. When the service was over nobody offered him food or shelter, but as he started down the long road with a breaking heart, the colored janitor asked him to share his humble meal in a nearby shanty.

Years passed. The young exhorter became Bishop Marvin of world-wide reputation, and after a full generation he once more stood in that spot to dedicate a great country church. The whole com-

munity was assembled; it was a tremendous event in their lives. When the service was ended, many crowded about offering lavish hospitality, but the Bishop waved them all aside, and called the old colored janitor saying, "When I was here years ago I was none too good for you, and I am none too good for you today."
—*Christian Life and Faith*

297 Just To Be Tender (I)

Just to be tender, just to be true,
Just to be loving, just living anew;
Just to be holy, just to be clean,
Trusting my Saviour, on Him to lean.

Just to be steady, just to be free,
Just to be ready His power to see;
Just to be happy, just to be right,
Just to be joyful, walking in light,

Just to be winning souls that are lost,
Telling of Jesus who paid the cost;
Just to be serving, just to be real;
Leading the helpless His grace to feel.

Just to be waiting Jesus from Heaven,
Just to be having His victory giv'n;
Kindness to show, wrongs to forget,
Victorious prayer, none will regret.
—Joseph T. Larson

KNOWLEDGE

298 Halfway Mark of Knowledge

Studies have shown that the halfway point of all human knowledge is located less than ten years ago; that is man's knowledge has doubled within the past decade. *Every 60 seconds, 2000 typewritten pages are added to man's knowledge and the material produced every 24 hours takes one person 5 years to read.*

299 US Spending For Knowledge

Americans spend $11.6 billion for books, magazine and newspapers in 1976. This against $5.9 billion in 1967.

A staggering $17.5 billion was also spent for radios, TV, records and musical instruments. This against $8.5 billion in 1967.

300 Five Million Words A Second

One recent development is a memory that can operate so fast that it can assimilate into permanent storage 5 million words per second. Since the Bible has 850,000 words, this memory is capable of assimilating the entire Bible 6 times in one second and bring it again, word by word, any passage, any verse, any place, at a command, in 200-billionth of a second. No errors are allowed. Running at that rate, each unit has to pass a test in which it runs 24 hours without a single error.

LEISURE

301 Spending Statistics
Americans spend $146 billion for recreation in 1976, itemized as follows:

Equipment	$77 billion
Travels	$55 billion
Foreign Travels	$11 billion
Cottages & Lots	$3 billion

This figure soared to $160 billion in 1977. Leisure-time expenditures can be expected to double every 8-9 years.

This U.S. phenomenon has been sparked by longer paid vacation, more three-day weekends, and rising family incomes.

302 "Take It Easy"
Dr. Margaret Mead, distinguished anthropologist and author, made a very interesting observation in an address not long ago. She pointed out that for a long time it was the universal custom to say on parting: "Good-bye," which is a shortened form of "God be with you." Today it is quite common instead to say: "Take it easy."

—*Pulpit Digest*

303 Department of Leisure
Social scientists tell us that a "work-less world" is just around the corner. Life in the world of tomorrow is pictured as having much leisure in it. Says Professor P.E. Vandall of the University of Windsor, "The 20-hour week is only 10 years away." The Southern California Research Council predicts that, by 1985, the typical American will have to work only six months a year to maintain his present standard of living.

R. F. Norden, in his book entitled "*The New Leisure*, says, "Some social scientists forsee the time, perhaps in the next 25 or even 10 years, when people constituting 2 percent of our population can do the necessary work to provide food and consumer goods for the remaining 98 percent; when state governments will establish departments of leisure to balance departments of labor."

—*Christian Victory*

LIBERAL THEOLOGY

304 The Issues
The Modernist-Fundamentalist controversy was based on:
1. virgin birth

2. deity
3. substitutionary atonement
4. bodily resurrection
5. second coming of Christ
6. inerrant authority of Scripture

305 To Celebrate Eve's Disobedience

"Eve's eating of the apple in the garden of Eden was the first free act of the human race. We ought to recognize that act. We ought to celebrate Eve. She began the .process of freedom." So stated the Reverend Patricia Budd Kepler, director of ministerial studies at Harvard Divinity School.

Speaking to the Western New York Presbytery, Reverend Kepler said that the expulsion of Adam and Eve from paradise into reality was God's way of giving birth to people. The minister went on to say that this made sin possible "because sin comes with freedom and choice."

—*Pastor's Manual*

306 Nothing Left But The Covers

A certain clergyman was called by a church to become its pastor. Having been strongly influenced by critical scholars who down-grade portions of the Scripture as myths, he himself doubted the authenticity of the whole Bible.

About two years after his coming, the pastor visited one of his members who was very sick. When he learned that the man had a terminal illness, he suggested, "Perhaps you would like me to read and pray for you?" "Yes," replied the man as he took his Bible and handed it to the minister. When he opened it, he was somewhat shocked at what he saw. Many of the pages were torn away, some of the chapters were missing, and a number of verses were actually cut! It was a terribly mangled volume.

Reluctantly the pastor asked, "Haven't you got a better Bible than this?" The dying man replied, "When you came to our church, I believed the entire Book. But as soon as you told us that certain sections were not true, I removed them. When you said that some stories were probably fiction and referred to them as fables, I tore them out. I think if I had another year under your teaching, I would have nothing but two covers left."

—P.R. Van Gorder

307 Edinburgh Conference's Fatal Flaw

One of the most appealing slogans to come out of an ecumenical gathering in this country is this one which appeared in 1947: "Partners in Obedience."

The phrase is compelling, but it is important to strip away the wrappings and examine what is inside.

In the case of the above slogan, one must go back to the truly significant World Missionary Conference which met in Edinburgh in 1910. At the helm of that meeting was John R. Mott, a dedicated, evangelical, Methodist layman with a passion to evangelize the world.

One aspect of the Edinburgh conference was a fatal spiritual flaw. In order to secure the participation of every individual and get on with the missionary task, a decision was made to exclude discussion of "questions of doctrine or church policy with regard to which the churches or societies taking part in the conference differ among themselves."

As a matter of fact, most of the participants at the Edinburgh conference were conservative, evangelical Christians. But by that ill-advised decision, liberalism became pervasive in the direction of the movement.

It is significant that the ecumenical movement grew out of a desire to cooperate in carrying out the great commission.

—*Bible Expositor*

LIFE, CHRISTIAN

308   How He Lived

Not, how did he die?
    But, how did he live?
Not, what did he gain?
    But, what did he give?

These are the merits
    To measure the worth
Of a man as man,
    Regardless of birth.

Not, what was his station?
    But, had he a heart?
And how did he play
    His God-given part?

Was he ever ready
    With word of good cheer
To bring a smile,
    To banish a tear?

Not what was his church?
    Nor, what was his creed?
But had he befriended
    Those really in need?

Not, what did the sketch
    In the newspaper say?
But, how many were sorry
    When he passed away?

               —Selected

309   My Influence

My Life shall touch a dozen lives
    Before this day is done,
Leave countless marks of good or ill,
    E'er sets the evening sun.
This, the wish I always wish,
    The prayer I always pray;
Lord, may my life help other lives,
    It touches by the way.

               —Selected

310   The Knight's Pledge

In his "Idylls of the King", Tennyson gives the knight's pledge: "Live pure, speak truth, right the wrong, follow the king; else wherefore born?"

Is not this a good motto for the Christian? He must live a pure life, which means a holy one; he certainly must speak the truth and do what he can to right conditions that are wrong. Above all, he must folllow the King, the Lord Jesus Christ, the Author and Finisher of our faith.

LITERATURE, CHRISTIAN

311   Only One-Half Percent

It has been calculated that all missionaries in the world combined reach fewer than ½% of the heathen in the world by word-of-mouth. How can we reach the 99½% without? To reach the 2,500,000,000 unevangelized we must employ prayer-backed Gospel literature.

          —The Bible Friend

312   Bunyan Saved By A Tract

It was Leigh Richmond, who dropped a tract on the pavement in England and prayed that a bad man would pick it up.

A bad man did pick it up. He carried the tract with him to prison and he was converted, and he wrote *Pilgrim's Progress*, which turned millions to rightusness. He was John Bunyan.

          —Selected

313   Epigram

●There are only two powers in the world—the sword and the pen; and, in the end, the former is always conquered by the latter.

          —Napoleon

●"Give me twenty-six lead soldiers, and I'll conquer the world," said Benjamin Franklin. "The pen is mightier than the sword."

LONELINESS

314 "Silent Partner" For Women Drivers

Some enterprising manufacturer has invented and is selling "A Silent Partner" for unattended ladies driving alone in a car at night. This "Silent Partner" is a "made-to-order" companion, even if he doesn't speak to her. He is lifesize and "infatable" and he sits next to the girl in the front seat, so she doesn't appear to be alone.

315 Daughter's Death Kills Father

A heart-rending story was reported by the press, telling of a young father who shot himself in a telephone booth. James Lee had called a Chicago newspaper and told a reporter he had sent the paper a manila envelope containing the story of his suicide.

The reporter frantically traced the call, but it was too late! When the police arrived, the young man was slumped in the booth with a bullet through his head.

In one of his pockets, they found a child's crayon drawing, much faded and worn. On it was written, "Please leave this in my coat pocket. I want to have it buried with me." The drawing was signed in a childish print by his little blonde daughter, Shirley who had perished in a fire just five months before.

Lee had been so grief-stricken that he asked total strangers to attend his daughter's funeral so she would have a nice service. He said there was no family to attend because Shirley's mother had been dead since the child was two years old.

The grieving father could not stand the loneliness or the loss, so he took his life.

—Selected

316 Walking 12,000 Miles For Home

In New York in the spring of 1927, Lillian Alling, a young servant, became very homesick and decided to return to her family in Russia, although it meant she would have to walk the 12,000 miles because she had saved only $100 and would not accept lifts from strangers. Equipped with maps, a knapsack and an iron rod for protection, the frail girl passed through Chicago, Winnipeg, British Columbia, the Yukon and Alaska, arriving in Nome, the halfway mark for her epic journey, in July 1929.

Not only had Lillian endured untold hardships, but she had lost her dog. After having been her pet and companion for a year, the little fellow had died back in the Yukon and she, unable to part with him, had stuffed his skin with the aid of a trapper and was carrying his body with her in a cart.

Soon after leaving Nome, she was seen approaching Cape Prince of Wales and that was the last time anyone on this continent is known to have seen or heard of her. She had apparently reached the Cape, as she had planned, obtained a boat and rowed across the 36 miles of Bering Strait to Siberia.

—Freling Foster

LOVE

317 Longest Love Letter

The longest—and simplest—love letter ever written was the work of a Parisan painter named Marcel de Leclure in 1875. The addressed was Magdalene de Villalore, his aristocratic light of love. The missive contained the phrase *"jevous aime"* "I Love You" 1,875,000 times—a thousand times the calendar years of the date. The prodigious lover did not pen the letter with his own hand. He hired a scribe. A lazy type could have instructed the secretary: "Write the amatory sentence 1,875,000 times." But Leclure was too entranced with the sound of the three words. He dictated it word for word and had the hired man repeat it verbatim. All in all therefore the phrase was uttered orally and in writing 5,625,000 times — before it reached its destination. Never was love made manifest by as great an expenditure of time and effort.

—Robert Ripley

318 Mother Charges Nothing

A mother found under her place one morning at breakfast a bill made out by her small son, Bradley, aged eight — Mother owes Bradley: for running errands, 25 cents; for being good, 10 cents; for taking music lessons, 15 cents; for extras, 5 cents. Total, 55 cents.

Mother smiled but made no comment. At lunch Bradley found the bill under his plate with 55 cents and another piece of paper neatly folded like the first. Opening it he read — Bradley owes Mother: for nursing him through scarlet fever, nothing; for being good to him, nothing; for clothes, shoes and playthings, nothing; for his playroom, nothing; for his meals, nothing. Total: nothing.

—Selected

319 Feeding One Another In Heaven

A man had just arrived in Heaven, told Peter how grateful he was to be in such a glorious place, and asked Peter to give him one glimpse into Hades in order that he might appreciate his good fortune even more. This Peter did.

In Hades he saw a long table extending as far as the eye could reach, laden down with the most delicious of all varieties of foods. But everyone around the table was starving to death. When asked for an explanation, Peter said, "Everyone is required to take food from the table only with four-foot long chopsticks. They are so long that no one can reach the food from the table to his mouth, and therefore each one is dying of starvation."

Quickly they returned to Heaven, and behold, the new arrival saw an identical table, laden down with identical foods, but everyone around the table was happy and well fed. Then he said to Peter: "With what do they take the food from the table?" and Peter answered, "Only with four-foot long chopsticks." At that the new arrival inquired: "Then why are all those in Hades starving to death while all those up here are so well fed and happy?" Whereupon Peter replied: "In Heaven we feed each other."

—Harry C. Mabry

320 Epigram

●Anybody can be a heart specialist. The only requirement is loving somebody.   —Angie Papadakis

●Those who love deeply never grow old; they may die of old age, but they die young.   —Ladies' Home Journal

●The loneliest place in the world is the human heart when love is absent.

—E.C. McKenzie

●Love is not blind — it sees more, not less. But because it sees more, it is willing to see less.   —Rabbi Julius Gordon

●Love may not make the world go around, but it sure makes the trip worthwhile.   —Bits & Pieces

●It is no chore for me to love the whole world. My only real problem is my neighbor next door.   —The Defender

●About 200 years ago one of our well-known encyclopedias discussed the word "atom" with the use of only four lines. But five pages were devoted to a discussion of "love."

In a recent edition of the same encyclopedia five pages were given to the word "atom"; "love" was omitted.

●He drew a circle that shut me out:
Heretic, rebel, a thing to flout;
But love and I had a mind to win;
We drew a circle and took him in.

—Selected

LOVE, BROTHERLY

321 Charles Lamb's Sacrifice

Into the life of Charles Lamb there came a deep attachment to a woman, but he willingly forsook marriage when he saw the need of his own family. Brother, son, and husband, he became the guardian angel of that home, and especially of his sister Mary, who was at times mentally deranged.

After she had stabbed her mother to death in one of her mad moments, Charles Lamb stripped himself for his sister Mary as Jonathan stripped himself for David; and for eight and thirty years he watched over her with a tender solicitude. A friend tells how he would sometimes see the brother and sister walking hand in hand across the field to the old asylum, both their faces bathed in tears. A sad story, and yet a grand story. Charles Lamb had his place in his home, and it was never left empty.

—C. E. Macartney

322 Legend Of Two Hebrew Brothers

There is a beautiful Hebrew legend of two brothers who lived side by side on adjoining lands. One was the head of a large family, the other lived alone. One night, the former lay awake and thought: "My brother lives alone, he has not the companionship of wife and children to cheer his heart as I have. While he sleeps, I will carry some of my sheaves into his field."

At the same hour, the other brother reasoned: "My brother has a large family, and his necessities are greater than mine. As he sleeps, I will put some of my sheaves on his side of the field." Thus the two brothers went out, each carrying out his purposes and each laden with sheaves—and met at the dividing line. There they embraced.

Years later, at the very place stood the Jerusalem temple, and on the very spot of their meeting stood the temple's altar.

LOVE FOR GOD

323 When Excess Is Good

On his 99th birthday, Carl J. Printz, for many years the Commissioner from Sweden to Canada, stepped quickly on to the television stage, his keen eyes expressing wisdom and understanding of his years. He was asked for rules by which such a long and useful life might be achieved. He replied:

"I would suggest one definite rule and that is, one must be temperate in all things." Then he added quickly,"perhaps I should say all but one, for in the Bible you can read the commandments to love the Lord with all your heart, soul and mind, and your neighbor as yourself. These are the only things we can rightly do to excess."

324 He Chooses To Be Seraphim

It is said that the young son of Bishop Berkeley once asked him the question, "Papa, what do the words, 'Cherubim and seraphim' mean?"

The bishop took time to tell the little questioner that cherubim was a Hebrew word meaning knowledge, and the word seraphim stood for flame, explaining that it is commonly supposed the cherubim are angels that excell in knowledge and the seraphim are those who excell in love for God.

"Then I hope," the boy said, "that when I die I will be a seraphim. I'd a lot rather love God than to know everything."

—Evangelistic Illustration

325 When Pastor Couldn't Give Benediction

On one occasion Mr. Flavel preached·

from these words: "If any man love not the Lord Jesus Christ, let him be anathema, maranatha." The discourse was unusually solemn, particularly the explanation of the words anathema, maranatha—"cursed with a curse, cursed of God, with a bitter and grievous curse." When he rose to pronounce the benediction he paused, and said, "How shall I bless this whole assembly, when every person in it, who loveth not the Lord Jesus Christ, is anathema, maranatha?"

The solemnity of this address deeply affected the audience, and one gentleman, a person of rank, was so much overcomed by his feelings, that he fell senseless to the floor. Fifty-three years afterwards the memory of this sermon was blessed to the conversion of a man who had heard it, named Luke Short, in his hundredth year of age.

—Selected

LUKEWARMNESS

326 The Devil's Strategy

The Devil held a great anniversary, at which his emissaries were convened to report the results of their several missions. "I let loose the wild beasts of the desert." said one, "on a caravan of Christians; and their bones are now bleaching on the sands." "What of that?" said the Devil, "their souls were all saved."

"For ten years, I tried to get a single Christian asleep," said a third; "and I succeeded, and left him so." Then the Devil shouted, and the night stars of hell sang for joy.

—Martin Luther

327 Young Gandhi With Christian Family

While attending a university in London, Mahatma Gandhi became almost convinced that the Christian religion was the one true, supernatural religion in the world. Upon graduation, and still seeking evidence that would make him a committed Christian, young Gandhi accepted employment in East Africa and for seven months lived in the home of a family who were members of an evangelical Christian church. As soon as he discovered that fact he decided that here would be the place to find the evidence he sought.

But as the months passed and he saw the casualness of their attitude toward the cause of God, heard them complain when they were called upon to make sacrifice for the kingdom of God and sensed their general religious apathy, Gandhi's interest turned to disappointment. He said in his heart, "No, it is not the one true, supernatural religion I had hoped to find. A good religion, but just one more of the many religions in the world."

—Evangelical Illustration

328 The Frozen Ship

We read of a vessel discovered a century ago, among the icebergs of the Arctic ocean, with the captain frozen as he was making his last entry in the log-book. The crew were discovered, some in their hammocks and some in the cabin, all frozen to death. The last date in the log-book showed that for thirteen years that vessel had been moving among the icebergs, "a drifting sepulchre, manned by a frozen crew." Are there not churches in a like condition?

MAN

329 Worth Of A Man

It has been estimated that the chemical contents (inorganic compounds) of a 150 lbs. man is worth:

—in the 1930s 98c
—in the 1960s $3.50
—in the 1970s $5.60

Over 60% of the body weight is water, which would be free.

330 Education Raises Man's Value

How much is a man worth? According to the Institute of Life Insurance, it all depends upon the education he gets.

The Institute values a man in terms of potential life income. A grade school graduate can expect to earn in a normal lifetime $219,000; a high school graduate, $303,000; a college graduate, $444,000.

331 Life's Key Words

1 - 20 years—learning
20 - 30 years—ladies
30 - 40 years—living
40 - 50 years—liberty
50 - 60 years—leisure
60 - 70 years—living

—*Speaker's Sourcebook*

MARRIAGES

332 Marrying Each Other 27 Times

To protest against the increasing number of divorces, James and Mary Grady of Illinois married each other—again and again—for 27 times between 1964-69.

They have gone through the ceremonies in 25 different states, 3 times in a day, twice in an hour, and twice over TV.

333 Married People Live Longer

According to insurance statistics, the death rate for married men aged 25 to 34 is 1.5 per thousand; for single men it is twice as high—more than 3.5 per thousand.

The difference is greater as men grow older: In the 35 to 44 group, the death rate for married men is 3.1 per thousand; for unmarried it is 8.3.

Among all women, the mortality rate for single females is almost twice that of women who are or have been married.

Which could mean that the moral is: *Better wed than dead.*

—New York Times

334 Grade School Boy Weds Teacher

From the Philippines comes this report: A fourth grader, Thomas Bautista, 14, was married to a widowed teacher by the Mayor at the town hall.

The bride, Julia N. Sumaguit, mother of four, is from the hometown of President Marcos. Her eldest is a boy about the same age as her new husband.

Mrs. Bautista teaches at Tibagan elementary school where her husband is enrolled. She was assigned there after passing a competitive test for teachers. According to Bautista's teacher-in-charge, Silvestre Mariano, the young bridegroom, "is a bright boy and ranks first in his class."

Mariano, who was among the wedding sponsors said Mrs. Bautista had confided to him she was willing to see her husband through school "for as long as he wishes to study."

335 Speeding Up "March"

The Wedding March has been so distorted that its composer would have difficulty recognizing it, says musicologist Maurice Zam.

The March comes from Wagner's opera Lehengrin, and the tempo of it as indicated by Wagner was andante con moto. This means "faster than a walk." It should be a joyful rhythmic swing toward the altar. Instead, the wedding March today is played so slowly that only an acrobat could keen his balance in the promenade up the aisle. Better keyed for a murderer in his walk of the last mile toward legal extinction, it has become the most agonizing march in the history of civilized man.

Wagner's directions were siegreicher mut, which means courageous spirit, and schreit voran, which means advance forward. "A courageous spirit," Zam concludes, "is the mood and tempo which should motivate anyone getting married."

The cure? It involves the reformation of all future organists and musicians so that they play a wedding march andante con moto, meaning "Let's speed this thing up and get on to the main business, which is a happy honeymoon."

—Frank Scully

MARTYRDOM

336 The Catacombs

During the years of the martyrs Christians fled into the underground caverns outside Rome in almost 600 miles of molelike tunnels.

Ten generations of Christians were buried in the catacombs during the approximate 300 years of suppression. No one knows the exact number, but archaeologists estimate between 1,750,000 and 4,000,000 Christians were interred in the dark tunnels.

Inscriptions of Scripture can still be seen on the catacomb walls. One of the most frequent inscriptions is the sign of the fish. But the inscription which best describes their faith says: "The Word of God is not bound."

—Selected

337 Martyrdoms Past And Present

It is estimated that more than 50 million Christians died for their faith in the Dark Ages. It is estimated that a million Christians died for their faith when the Communists seized China. Unnumbered thousands died as martyrs in the revolutions and civil wars in Africa recently.

338 More Last Words Of Martyrs

*Henry Vos—"If I had twin heads, they should all be off for Christ."

*Castilla Rupea—"Though you throw my body down off this steep hill. yet will my soul mount upwards again."

*John Buisson—"I shall have a double jail delivery: out of my sinful flesh and out of the loathsome dungeon I have long lain in."

*Taylor—"Now lack I but two steps, and I am even at my Father's house."

*Carpenter—"All Bavaria is not as dear to me as my wife and children. but, for Christ's sake, I gladly forsake them.

MIDDLE AGE

339 Prayer For The Middle-Aged

Lord, Thou knowest better than I myself that I am growing older and will some day be old. Keep me from that fatal habit of thinking I must say something on every subject and on every occasion. Release me from craving to straighten out everyone's affairs. Make me thoughtful, but not moody; helpful, but not boosy.

With my vast store of wisdom, it seems a pity not to use it all, but Thou knowest, Lord, that I want a few friends at the end.

Keep my mind free from the recital of endless details, give me wings to get to the point. Seal my lips on my aches and pains. They are increasing and love of rehearsing them is becoming sweeter as the years go by.

I dare not ask for grace enough to enjoy the tales of others' pains, but help me to endure them with patience.

I dare not ask for improved memory, but for a growing humility and a lessening cocksureness when my memory seems to clash with the memories of others. Teach me the glorious lesson that occasionally I may be mistaken.

Keep me reasonable, sweet. I do not want to be a saint: some of them are so hard to live with, but a sour old person is one of the crowning works of the devil. Give me the ability to see good things in unexpected places and talents in unex-pected people. Give me the grace to tell them so.

—Now

340 The Youth Of Old Age

Victor Hugo, titan of French literature, was once called upon to comfort a friend who had arrived at his 50th birthday and was depressed at the idea of growing old.

"You should rejoice, my friend," Hugo told him, "that you have escaped your forties, which are the old age of youth, and have at last arrived at the age of fifty, which is the youth of old age."

—Selected

341 Epigram

●Middle Age is that perplexing time of life when we hear two voices calling us, one saying, "Why not?" and the other, "Why bother?" —*Last Things First*

●The first half of our lives is ruined by our parents and the second half by our children. —Clarence S. Darrow

●"Our generation never got a break. When we were young, they taught us to respect our elders, and now that we're older, they tell us to listen to the youth."

●When I was a boy I used to do what my father wanted. Now I have to do what my boy wants. My problem is: when am I going to do what I want?

—Sam Levenson

●If a middle-aged school superinten-dent could only sell his experience for half what it cost him, he could live in retirement and luxury.

MISSIONS

342 "We Are Everywhere"

The growth of Christianity in the early centuries was phenomenal. By mid 2nd century, an apologist said,"We are every-where. We are in your towns and in your cities; we are in your army and navy; we are in your palaces; we are in the senate; we are more numerous than anyone."

By AD 300, the church was spreading so fast that it appeared the entire civilized world could be evangelized by AD 500.

But Constantine decreed that every one in the empire was already Christian. And slowly the idea prevailed of a division between laity and clergy, for pagans could not evangelize nor know how. And Christianity's movement was checked.

343 Travel Scenes And Paul

The Apostle Paul was perhaps one of the greatest travelers of his day. He visited many lands, and saw many new scenes in different countries. When he returned he wrote a good deal; his Epistle were widely read by the early churches. And yet, in all the writings of the apostle, there is not one line that is descriptive of the scenery of the countries through which he passed; not a line telling of the wonders of the architecture of his day; not a line describing the customs of the people.

Is not this singular? There is a reason for it. The apostle was "blind." As he traveled about he was blind to all else but one thing. On the way to Damascus, when he met the Lord Jesus, He was blinded by the vision of His great glory, and from that time he could see nothing but Him and tell of nothing but His Gospel.

—R. A. Jaffray

344 Go Ye, But How Far?

According to the latest available statistics the ratio of Protestant missionaries to population in strategic world areas shows:

1,448 Ministers per million people in the United States.

56 Missionaries per million people in Africa.

30 Missionaries per million people in South America.

20 Missionaries per million people in Korea.

15 Missionaries per million people in India.

Moreover, much of Europe with its 480 million people is largely unevangelized. And virtually all Communist-controlled countries are closed to missions work.

345 Famous Unwritten Letter To Paul

This is a letter that could have been written to the Apostle Paul had he applied for missionary service under some of today's modern missionary boards:

Rev. Saul (Apostle) Paul
Independent Missionary
Corinth, Greece

Dear Mr. Paul:

We recently received an application from you for service under our Board. It is our policy to be as frank and open-minded as possible with all of our applicants. We have made an exhaustive survey of your case. To be plain, we are surprised that you have been able to "pass" as a bonafide missionary. We are told that you are afflicted with a severe eye trouble. This is certain to be an insuperable handicap to an effective ministry. We require 20-20 vision.

Do you think it seemly for a missionary to do part-time secular work? We heard that you are making tents on the side. In a letter to the Church at Philippi you admitted that they were the only church supporting you. We wonder why?

Is it true that you have a jail record? Certain brethren report that you did two years' time at Caesarea, and was imprisoned at Rome.

You made so much trouble for the

businessmen at Ephesus that they refer to you as "the man who turned the world upside down." Sensationalism has no place in missions! We also deplore the lurid over-the-wall episode at Damascus. We are appalled at your obvious lack of conciliatory behavior. Diplomatic men are not stoned and dragged out of the city gate, or assaulted by furious mobs. Have you ever suspected that gentler words might gain you more friends? I enclose a copy of Dalius Carnagus' book, "How to Win Jews and Influence Greeks."

In one of your letters you refer to yourself as Paul the Aged. Our new mission policies do not anticipate a surplus of elderly recipients. We understand, too, that you are given to fantasies and dreams. At Troas, you saw, "A man of Macedonia" and at another time you were "caught up into the third heaven" and even claimed that "the Lord stood by" you. We reckon that more realistic and practical minds are needed in the task of world evangelism.

You have written many letters to churches where you have formerly been pastor. In one of these letters, you accused a church member of living with his father's wife, and you caused the whole church to feel badly and the poor fellow was expelled.

Your ministry has been far too flightly to be sucessful. First Asia Minor, then Macedonia, then Greece, then Italy, and now you are talking about a wild-goose chase to Spain. Concentration is more important than dissipation of one's powers. You cannot win the whole world by yourself! You are just one little Paul. In a recent sermon you said, "God forbid that I should glory in anything save the Cross of Christ." It seems to us that you also ought to glory in our heritage, our denominational program, the unified budget.

Your sermons are much too long for the time. At one place you talked until after midnight and a young man was so sleepy that he fell out of the window and broke his neck. Nobody is saved after the first 20 minutes. "Stand up, speak up, and shut up," is our advice.

Dr. Luke reports that you are a thin little man, bald, frequently sick, and always so agitated over your churches that you sleep very poorly. He reports that you pad around the house, praying half the night. A healthy mind in a robust body is our ideal for all applicants. A good night's sleep will give you zest and zip so that you wake up full of zing!

You wrote recently to Timothy that you had "fought a good fight." Fighting is hardly a recommendation for a missionary. No fight is a good fight. Jesus came not to bring a sword, but peace. You boast that "I fought with wild beasts of Ephesus." What on earth do you mean?

It hurts me to tell you this, brother Paul, but in all of the 25 years of my experience, I have never met a man so opposite to the requirements of our Foreign Mission board. If we accepted you, we would break every rule of modern missionary practice.

Most Sincerely yours,
J. Flavius Fluffyhead, Sec.
Foreign Missions Board

JFF: hmh

346 If Everyone Tithe

If the Protestant people of America alone were tithing their income we could easily evangelize the entire world and put a copy of the Bible into the hands of every heathen on earth inside of ten years. According to government statistics, we are spending annually in this country six hundred dollars for luxuries for every dollar we spend for missions. We spend in America more for tobacco in a single year than both the United States and Canada have spent for missions since white man discovered America.

—Oscar Lowery

MONEY

347 A Dollar Speaks

Money talks, we have been told since childhood. Listen to this dollar speak: "You hold me in your hand and call me yours. Yet may I not as well call you mine. See how easily I rule you? To gain me, you would all but die. I am impersonal as rain, essential as water. Without me, men and institutions would die. Yet I do not hold the power of life for them; I am futile without the stamp of your desire. I go nowhere unless you send me. I keep strange company. For me, men mock, love, and scorn character. Yet, I am appointed to the service of saints, to give education to the growing mind and food to the starving bodies of the poor. My power is terrific. Handle me carefully and wisely, lest you become my servant, rather than I yours."

— Ray O. Jones

348 Unique Bank Note Microbe

Dr. Watkinson tells us that some years ago two scientists of Vienna made a series of bacteriological experiments on a number of bank notes which had been in circulation for some time. The result of their researches was sufficiently startling.

On each bank note they discovered the presence of 19,000 microbes of disease — some of tuberculosis, some of diphtheria, and some of erysipelas. More than that, they found one bacillus peculiar to the bank note — the bank note microbe, so to speak, because it is found nowhere else. It thrives and fattens and multiplies on the peculiar paper of which a bank note is made. Is there not a parable here?

349 He Jumped Overboard That Same Moment

Augustine Birrell was Secretary of State for Ireland in the early days of the Asquith administration, and was among

the most brilliant essayists of the closing days of the nineteenth century. He and his wife were driving through London one day and came to a mansion of magnificent proportion that took their breath away.

Mrs. Birrell looked at it enviously, asked whose it was, and remarked how happy the owner must be to possess such a place. Mr. Birrell said it belonged to 'Barney Barnato', one of the world's richest men and partner with Cecils Rhodes. 'Perhaps,' he added, 'for all his wealth he is not happy.'

In recording the incident later, Mr. Birrell stated that it was almost at that hour that Barnato jumped overboard from a boat coming from South Africa to end his unhappy life. Wealth does not bring happiness.

350 Epigram

●Millionaires who laugh are rare. My experience is that wealth is apt to take the smiles away. — Andrew Carnegie

●Happiness is a two way station between too much and too little.
—Channing Pollock

●Some of us do not believe we are having a good time unless we are doing something we can't afford.

●Money will buy a fine dog, but only love will make him wag his tail.

●Money makes strangers.
—Japanese Proverb

●The poorest man I know is the man who has nothing but money.
—John D. Rockefeller, Jr.

●It is known that Lincoln had no great admiration for mere financial success. "Financial success," he once said, "is purely metallic. The man who gains it has four metallic attributes: gold in his palm, silver on his tongue, brass in his face, and iron in his heart!"

●Upon the statue of Joseph Brotherton is the inscription, "A man's riches consist not in the amount of his wealth, but in the fewness of his wants."

●The late Robert Horton said the greatest lesson he learned from life was that people who set their minds and hearts on money are equally disappointed whether they get it or whether they don't.

351 Babel's Last Word

According to tradition, the very last word uttered before the tongues were confused at Babel was the word "Sack" or bag. Money-consciousness apparently started early.

MOTHER

352 To Mother

You painted no Madonnas
  On chapel walls in Rome,
But with a touch diviner
  You lived one in your home.

You wrote no lofty poems
  That critics counted art,
But with a nobler vision
  You lived them in your heart.

You carved no shapeless marble
  To some high-souled design,
But with a finer sculpture
  You shaped this soul of mine.

You built no great cathedrals
  That centuries applaud,
But with a grace exquisite
  Your life cathedraled God.

Had I the gift of Raphael,
  Or Michelangelo,
Oh, what a rare Madonna
My mother's life would show!
          —Thomas W. Fessenden

353 The Statue Of Liberty

For the past ninety years the majestic statue "Liberty Enlightening the World" has towered above Bedlow Island, near the entrance to New York Harbor, as a symbol of the freedom which we enjoy here in America.

The famous sculptor, Bartholdi, gave twenty years of devoted effort to the work, personally superintending the raising of the subscription of $4,000,000 with which the French nation gave the statue to the United States. When the subscriptions lagged, Bartholdi pledged his own private fortune to defray the running expenses and practically impoverished himself over the work.

At the start, when Bartholdi looked for a model whose form and features he could reproduce as "Liberty," he received much contradictory counsel. One of the leading art authorities advised him that the statue should depict "figures of thought which are grand in themselves." After examining outstanding heroes, Bartholdi chose as a model for the colossal masterpiece—his own mother.
          —Christian Victory

354 Baby's Footprints Toward Church

Near a church in Kansas, there can be seen in a cement sidewalk the prints of two baby feet with the toes pointing toward the Church. It was said that 20 years ago, when the sidewalk was being laid, a mother secured permission to stand her baby boy on the wet cement. The tracks are seen today plainly. The Mother had wanted her little boy to start aright.

355 Edison's Tribute To His Mother

I did not have my mother long, but she cast over me an influence which has lasted all my life. The good effects of her early training I can never lose. If it had not been for her appreciation and her faith in me at a critical time in my experience, I should never likely have become an inventor. I was always a careless boy, and with a mother of different mental calibre, I should have turned out badly. But her firmness, her sweetness, her goodness, were potent powers to keep me in the right path. My mother was the making of me. The memory of her will always be a blessing to me.

—Thomas A. Edison

356 Court Decides Mother Drowned First

In a New Orleans cemetery is a monument which has created much interest. It represents a ship in the midst of a storm-tossed sea; a mother and child clinging together on the vessel. On the base is an inscription saying they were drowned on July 4, 1900.

They were sole survivors of a large estate, and the question was under whose name should the estate be administered— the name of the mother or the daughter. The Court decided it should be in the name of the child, reckoning she went down *last*, because the mother would hold her in a place of safety to the end. A wonderful tribute to mother's love!

357 "Are You Hurt, My Son?"

A daring story has been told of a young Frenchman who loved a courtesan. This woman hated her lover's mother, and when, in his passion, he offered her any gift in return for her love, she answered: "Bring me then your mother's bleeding heart."

And he, in his madness, killed his mother and, plucking out her heart, hurried by night through the streets, carrying it to the cruel woman to whom he had given his soul. But as he went he stumbled and fell, and from the bleeding heart came an anxious voice: 'My son, are you hurt?' Not even murder could kill that mother's love; it lived on in the torn heart.

—*Ministers' Research Service*

358 One Glimpse Of Her In Prayer

Once I suddenly opened the door of mother's room, and saw her on her knees beside her chair, and heard her speak my name in prayer. I quickly and quietly withdrew, with a feeling of awe and reverence in my heart. Soon I went away from home to school, then to college, then into life's sterner duties.

But I never forgot that one glimpse of my mother at prayer, nor the one word— my name—which I heard her utter. Well did I know what I had seen that day was but a glimpse of what was going on every day in that sacred closet of prayer and the consciousness strengthened me a thousand times in duty, in danger, and in struggle. And when death came, at length and sealed those lips, the sorest sense of loss that I felt was the knowledge that no more would my mother be praying for me.

—J. R. Miller

359 Origin Of Mother's Day

The "Mother's Day" concept has a long history of religious connections which in modern times seem to have been predominantly Christian.

In ancient Greece, the idea of paying tribute to motherhood was given expression with a regular festival tantamount to mother worship. Formal ceremonies to Cybele, or Rhea, the "Great Mother of the Gods," were performed on the Ides of March throughout Asia Minor.

For Christianity, the concept seems to date back to establishment of England's "Mothering Sunday," a custom of the people which provided that one attend the mother church in which he was baptized on Mid-Lent Sunday. Gifts were to be offered at the altar to the church and to worshippers' mothers. The concept was divorced of any "mother worship," but nevertheless perpetuated its religious association.

U. S. observance of Mother's Day, too, has been characterized by church ties from the start. The first general observance of the occasion was in the churches of Philadelphia after Miss Anne Jarvis campaigned for a holiday for mothers more than 50 years ago.

　　　　　　　　　—*Christianity Today*

MUSIC, CHRISTIAN

360　Two Singing Religions

Judaism and Christianity are singing religions. Atheism is songless. It has nothing to sing about. The funeral notices of Robert Ingersoll, the noted agnostic, stated, "There will be no singing."

The psalm-singing of Christian martyrs going to their deaths in the arena alerted the Roman Empire to the fact that a new and revolutionary force was coming into being. When the pleasure-bent populace saw the Christians singing as they fearlessly entered the amphitheater where hungry lions awaited them, they were filled with awe.

Heaven is vibrant with song: "And they sing the song of Moses . . . and the song of the Lamb" (Rev. 15:3).

　　　　　　　　　—Walter B. Knight

361　Next To Theology

"Music is a fair and lovely gift of God which has often wakened and moved me to the joy of preaching . . . . Next after theology, I give to music the highest place and the greatest honor . . . . My heart bubbles up and overflows in response to music, which has so often refreshed me and delivered me from dire plagues."

　　　　　　　　　—Martin Luther

362　Favorite Hymns

At Indiana State Fair of 1971, in a poll taken of persons over 60 years old, the No. 1 favorite of Hymns was "How Great Thou Art." No. 2 favorite was "In the Garden," then "The Old Rugged Cross," then "Amazing Grace."

363　Epigram

●The requisites of a singer—a big chest, a big mouth, 90 per cent memory, 10 per cent intelligence, lots of hard work, and something in the heart.

　　　　　　　　　—Enrico Caruso

N

NARCOTICS

364 High Costs To Society

The cost of drug abuse to society in terms of crime, medical treatment, custodial care and loss of work amount to $10.3 billion a year. Heroin addiction accounts for over $6 billion of the total.

In addition, tobacco use costs society $6.7 billion a year, and alcoholism costs $32 billion annually.

365 Largest Pot Ever Seized

Miami, (AP)—Forty tons of a marijuana, valued at $24 million, were discovered on an island near Freeport, Bahamas, by federal agents on a search and rescue mission in August 16,1975.

It was believed to be the biggest marijuana seizure ever.

The marijuana was found on deep water key, about 15 miles southeast of Freeport, by agents searching the area for a downed helicopter. The search for the helicopter was called off, officials said.

The pot had been pressed into bricks and was staked eight feet high in burlap and plastic bags, agent said. They placed a value of $24 million on the dope.

366 Linkletter's Daughter

One of the tragic events of the last 1960's was what happened to Art Linkletter's daughter Diane. She had experimented with taking LSD, her father said, and had confided to him that the whole thing was ridiculous. Frightened by the experience and by the "bum trips" of friends, she vowed never to try LSD again. But hallucinations kept recurring until, depressed and afraid she was losing her mind, she leaped from her apartment to her death.

OCCULTISM

367 The Occult Boom

The occult boom prevalent today began with the wildfire spread of astrology. It then extended all the way from Satanism and Witchcraft to the edge of science.

One American in five expresses belief in astrology. Adherents of other movements include: Transcendental Meditation (4%), Yoga (3%), Charismatic Christianity (2%), Mysticism (2%), and Eastern Religions (1%).

368 Occult Books, Magazines, Films

Occult book sales doubled in the last four years. More than 800 different titles were involved. The occult movement has its own trade magazine called *Occult Trade Journal*. Doubleday's new book club of occult title zoomed to 100,000 membership in two years.

One of the busiest bookstores is Metaphysical Center in San Francisco, selling about $12,000 a month. It offered courses in palmistry, reincarnation, astral projection, numerology, and others.

Another bookstore sells ritual robes, amulets, incense, crystal balls, etc. The film *Exorcist* gained $70 million in a year, and the book by that title has 10,000,000 in print. Big colleges and universities offer credit courses on the occult.

369 More On The Movement

People are anxious to know what lies ahead, good or ill, and they are willing to pay for predictions.

Palm readers, psychics, numerologists, and other assorted diviners all have devout followings, as do Quija boards, the I Ching, and even the lowly tea leaves.

Astrology is enjoying an unprecedented boom according to the American Federation of Astrologers, which boasts a thousand active members.

Meanwhile, the gypsy fortunetellers have been joined by government-sponsored think tanks with names like Rand Corporation and Hudson Institute.

Industry and academia have lent respectability to stargazing with such organizations as the Commission on the Year 2000, sponsored by the prestigious American Association of Arts and Sciences, and the Institute for the Future, formed by a consortium of companies including Monsanto, Du Pont, and Chase Manhattan.

Abroad, the Club of Rome, the Futuribles of France, and Britain's Committee on the Next Thirty Years earnestly prognosticate.

Crystal balls have been replaced by computers, and instead of soothsayers making prophecies, we get systems theorists with world models, statistical projections, and extrapolated scenarios.

—*Prairie Overcomer*

370 10,000 Astrologers In U.S.

There are between 5,000 and 10,000 astrologers in the U.S. today. Astrologers' names fill two columns of the New York City yellow pages; the subject requires a full drawer in the Library of Congress and catalogue.

371 Some Statistics

The Buddhist sect called "Nichiren Shoshu" had 25,000 followers in the U.S. in 1965. In 1971 they number 200,000. A typical meeting is for all to be seated lotus-fashion, chanting the same words over and over again.

And Transcendental Meditation has 50,000 followers in the U.S. colleges alone.

372 One Million Americans

Satan worship and all forms of the occult is evident everywhere. It is estimated that there are at least 100 million Americans who dabble in some form of Black Magic.

In New Jersey, a young man was drowned by a group of his friends at his request, because he believed that a violent end would put him in command of forty legions of demons.

373 Willed To The Devil

A Finnish infidel died and left his farm

willed to the devil. The courts, after deliberating on such a ridiculous set of circumstances, decided the best way to carry out the wishes of the infidel was to permit the farmland to grow up in weeds and briars, to allow the house and barn to remain unpainted and to rot down, and to permit the soil to erode and wash away. The court said, "The best way to let Satan have it is to do nothing."

—*The Bible Friend*

OIL

374 Origin Of Oil

According to science: Oil was formed when the remains of primitive forms of life settled at the bottom of the seas. Large collections of these organisms turned into drops of oil, and as the floor of the sea was covered with sediments, the oil became trapped in pools.

The sediment took many shapes and formed different kinds of rock over the countless years. During this time the surface of the earth was subjected to buckling, uplifting, lowering, and sliding.

The sea bottom of prehistoric times may be thousands of feet above sea level today, due to uplifting. Or the ancient sea bottom may lie deep under today's dry land or ocean, due to lowering. It is the pools of oil trapped under rock, formed in prehistoric times, that man starts up and moves off on some errand. It is running on a part of the remains of billions upon billions of primitive organisms.

According to the Bible: God made it out of nothing at the touch of a word. Can it not be said that the omniscient Creator—having knowledge of all history and prophecy—located oil in the Middle East area for purposes of fulfilling end-time prophecies?

375 Where On Earth Are Oil?

The total supply of *unused* oil on earth

is estimated at 2 trillion barrels.

Oil deposits can be found throughout the world. One-half of this world's *potential* supply is either in the Arab-dominated Mideast or in the Communist world—Russia, China and the Eastern European countries. And about 80% are in the so-called "Oil axis poles," that is, the Gulf-Caribbean and the Mesopotamian-Persian Gulf areas.

376 World's Known Reserves

About three quarters of the world's *known* oil reserves are in the Middle East and North Africa. About one-half of total reserves are in the countries bordering the Persian Gulf.

The difficulties are: (1) Middle East supplies are not limitless, (2) Unexpected restrictions by oil producers, (3) Periodic surges and depressions in demand, (4) Delays in planned capacity, (5) Political relations between oil-producing and oil-consuming nations, and (6) New oil finds seem to be in more difficult terrains and environments, such as the Arctic and under oceans.

The major producing regions today include Texas and California in the United States, Alberta in Canada, Venezuela, the Middle East, Indonesia, Russia, North Africa, and the North Sea.

377 The Car That Started It All

A car wreck in 1907 changed the face of industry and is largely responsible for much of the pollution problem today. At the turn of the century the American automobile industry was in the throes of indecision. Two courses lay before them: to follow the well-defined path of steam propulsion, or to explore the lesser-known byway of gasoline power. Steam seemed to have the brightest future.

At the annual automobile races in Ormond, Florida, that fateful year, several gasoline cars had unsuccessfully tried to reach the 100-mph mark. Then Stanley Steamer, looking like a canoe turned upside down and nicknamed the "Flying Teakettle," took to the track. Fifty years later, driver Fred Marriott explained what happened:

"I quickly got up to 197 miles per hour, and the speed was rising fast when the car hit a slight bump. I felt it twist a little in the air. It rose off the beach and traveled a hundred feet through the air before it struck. I was thrown clear and pretty badly smashed. The machine was broken to pieces, with the boiler rolling and blowing steam like a meteor, for a mile down the beach."

In this manner the myth was born that a Steamer was just too fast to stay on the ground. Following came many legends about the car, which finally doomed its success and ushered in the age of the gasoline engine. Motor expert John Carlova feels this was the turning point of the industry. Perhaps if the course of the steam engine had been followed, our problems would not be so critical today.

—C.R. Hembree

OVERCOMING

378 They Took Away

They took away what should have
    been my eyes,
(But I remembered Milton's Paradise).
They took away what should have
    been my ears,
(Beethoven came and wiped away my
    tears).
They took away what should have
    been my tongue.
(But I had talked with God when I was
    young).
He would not let them take away my
    soul,
(Possessing that I still possess the
    whole).

—Helen Keller

379 Edison's Delight

Thomas Edison invented the phonograph at age 30, and he was almost totally deaf from childhood. He could hear only the loudest noises and shouts. This kind of delighted him, for he said, "A man who has to shout can never tell a lie!"

His other inventions: incandescent bulb, microphone, mimeograph, fluoroscope and movies.

380 Blind Milton's Books

Blind men seldom quote books, but it is not so with Milton. The prodigious power, readiness, and accuracy of his memory, as well as the confidence he felt in it, are proved by his setting himself, several years after he had become totally blind, to compose his *Treatise on Christian Doctrine*, which, made up as it is of Scriptural texts, would seem to require perpetual reference to the Sacred Volume.

A still more extraordinary enterprise was that of the Latin Dictionary— a work which, one would imagine, might easily wear out a sound pair of eyes.

After five years of blindness, he undertook these two vast works, along with *Paradise Lost*.

—Julius C. Hare

381 Crippled Lieutenant's Discovery

Lieutenant Maury rendered invaluable service to the sea-going nations of the earth, but would perhaps never have taken up the work for which his name is noted, had it not been for an accident that crippled him, and made it impossible for him to continue his career on the ocean. This is the way it came about:

For many years every sea captain was compelled to keep a log-book, in which he jotted down every day all facts of interest in his sailings, giving the direction of the wind and the currents, and other similar information. When the log-book was full, it was sent to Washington and stowed away among the records of the navigation department.

Young Lieutenant Maury, after he had been crippled, and so incapacitated for sea duty in the navy, went to Washington, got out the old log-books from the Navigation Bureau, sorted the data from every book and assigned all the information to its respective block on the ocean map which he was drafting.

Thus he discovered the "rivers in the ocean" and the rivers in the air, making charts by which the sailing time was reduced by twenty five per cent, and the expenses and perils were greatly reduced.

—*Missionary Review*

P

PASTOR

382 Number Of US Ministers

There are nearly 400,000 American Protestant clergymen, 250,000 pastors, 35,000 seminarians, and 35,000 missionaries.

In contrast, there are 58,000 American Catholic clergymen, 18,000 pastors, 17,000 seminarians and 7,000 missionaries.

383 What A Job!

"The pastor teaches, though he must solicit his own classes. He heals, though without pills or knife. He is sometimes a lawyer, often a social worker, something of an editor, a bit of a philosopher and entertainer; a salesman, a decorative piece for public functions, and he is supposed to be a scholar. He visits the sick, marries people, buries the dead, labors to console those who sorrow, and to admonish those who sin, and tries to stay sweet when chided for not doing his duty.

"He plans programs, appoints committees when he can get them; spends considerable time in keeping people out of each other's hair; between times he prepares a sermon and preaches it on Sunday to those who don't happen to have any other engagement. Then on Monday he smiles when some jovial chap roars, "'What a job—one day a week!'"

—Selected

384 A Letter From Paul

A certain church found itself suddenly without a pastor, and a committee was formed to search for a new man. In due course, the committee received a letter from a clergyman applying for the position. The letter went like this:

"Gentlemen: Understanding that your pulpit is vacant, I should like to submit my application. I am generally considered to be a good preacher. I have been a leader in most of the places I have served. I have also found time to do some writing on the side.

"I am over 50 years of age, and while my health is not the best, I still manage to get enough work done so as to please my parish.

"As for references, I am somewhat handicapped. I have never preached in any place for more than 3 years. And the churches I have preached in have generally been pretty small, even though they

113

were located in rather large cities. In some places I had to leave because my ministry caused riots and disturbances. Even where I stayed, I did not get along too well with other religious leaders in town, which may influence the kind of references these places will send you. I have also been threatened several times and even physically attacked. Three or four times I have gone to jail for witnessing to my convictions.

"Still, I feel sure I can bring vitality to your church even though I am not particularly good at keeping records. I have to admit I don't even remember all those whom I've baptized. However, if you can use me, I should be pleased to be considered."

Hearing the letter read aloud, the committee members were aghast. How could anyone think that a church like theirs could consider a man who was nothing but a troublemaking, absentminded, ex-jail-bird? What was his name?

"Well," said the chairman of the committee." the letter is simply signed . . . PAUL."

— *The Episcopalian*

385 **The Preacher's Wife**

There is one person in your church
   Who knows your preacher's life.
She's wept and smiled and prayed with
     him,
   And that's your preacher's wife!

She knows one prophet's weakest point,
   And knows his greatest power.
She's heard him speak in trumpet tone,
   In his great triumph hour.

She's heard him groaning in his soul,
   When bitter raged the strife,
As hand in his she knelt with him—
   For she's a preacher's wife!

The crowd has seen him in his strength.
   When gleamed his long drawn sword,
As underneath God's banner folds
   He faced the devil's horde.

But she knows deep within her heart
   That scarce an hour before,
She helped him pray the glory down
   Behind a closet door!

You tell your tales of prophets brave,
   Who walked across the world,
And changed the course of history,
   By burning words they hurled.

And I will tell how back of them
   Some women lived their lives,
Who wept with them and smiled
     with them—
   They were the preacher's wives!
          — *Selected*

386 **An Easy Job?**

You may think it quite an easy task,
   And just a pleasant life;
But really it takes a lot of grace
   To be a preacher's wife
She's supposed to be a paragon
   Without a fault in view,
A saint when in the parsonage
   As well as in the pew.

Her home must be a small hotel
   For folks that chance to roam,
And yet have peace and harmony—
   The perfect preacher's home!
Whenever groups are called to
     meet,
Her presence must be there,
And yet the members all agree
   She should live a life of prayer.

Though hearing people's burdens,
   Their grief both night and day,
She's supposed to spread but
     sunshine
   To those along the way.
She must lend a sympathetic ear
   To every tale of woe,
And then forget about it,
   Lest it to others go.

Her children must be models rare
   Of quietness and poise,
But still stay on the level
   With other girls and boys.
You may think it quite an easy task,

And just a pleasant life,
But really it takes a lot of grace
To be a preacher's wife!

—*Selected*

387 Praying For Pastor: A Thousand Strong

Dr. J. Wilbur Chapman in his first pastorate in Philadelphia was visited by a layman who frankly said to him: 'You are not a strong preacher. In the usual order of things you will fail here, but a little group of laymen have agreed to gather every Sunday morning and pray for you.' Dr. Chapman added: 'I saw that group grow to one thousand men gathered weekly to pray for this preacher.' Of course, he had great success. Almost any pastor would succeed if a group of leaders would thus back him up.

—*The Presbyterian*

388 Five Ways To Get Rid Of Pastor

1. Sit up front, smile, and say "Amen" every time he says something good. He will preach himself to death.

2. Pat him on the back and tell him what good work he is doing in the church and community. He will work himself to death.

3. Increase your offering to the church. He will suffer from shock.

4. Tell him you've decided to join the visitation group and help win souls for the Lord. He will probably suffer a heart attack.

5. Get the whole church to band together and pray for him. He will get so efficient that some other church will hear about him and give him a call. That will take him off your hands.

—*Selected*

389 A Pastor Tears Up His Bible

This is a true story. A man who was foreman on a construction job was noted for his vulgarity and ungodly disposition among the men who worked for him.

A Christian man on the job was grieved to hear so much cursing and vile language. One day he got up enough courage to speak to his foreman on the matter. He received this story from the lips of the man:

"I was once pastor of the First_____Church in this city. Some trouble arose in the congregation of such magnitude that there seemed to be no solution. I was so distraught and provoked that I did not know what to do. One Sunday morning I walked up to the pulpit and literally tore my Bible into shreds and threw it piece by piece at the congregation. Then I walked out of the pulpit and out of the church, vowing never to enter again. That's why I am so wicked today."

—*Gospel Herald*

390 I.O.U. Or U.O. Me?

The minister of a small Detroit church believed some practical joker was joshing him when I.O.U.'s began to appear in the collection plate. One Sunday night, weeks later, the collection included an envelope containing bills equal to the total of the I.O.U.'s.

After that, the parson could hardly wait to see what the amount the anonymous donor had promised. The range in contributions was from $5 to $15—apparently based on what the donor thought the sermon to be worth. And there came a Sunday when the collection plate brought a note reading, "U.O.Me $5."

391 Epigram

●The church elders in the little New Hampshire town had voted to keep their minister in spite of his radical tendencies. A visitor to the village, knowing their extremely narrow beliefs, commended one of the elders for having taken such a broad view.

"Broad view, nonsense!" retorted the elder. "We all know the dominie has dangerous ideas, but we'd rather have him here." The elder winked a shrewd eye. "If he wasn't here, he'd be somewhere else. There people might listen to him."

—Coronet

PERSEVERANCE

392 Creed Of Olympic Games

These words were spelled out in lights at the 18th Olympics at Tokyo in 1964:

"The most important thing in the Olympic Games is not to win but to take part; just as the most important thing in life is not the triumph but the struggle. The essential thing is . . . to have fought well."

393 Edison's Light Bulb

Edison did not give up when his first efforts to find an effective filament for the carbon incandescent lamp failed. He did countless experiments with countless kinds of materials. As each failed, he would toss it out the window. The pile reached to the second story of his house. Then he sent men to China, Japan, South America, Asia, Jamaica, Ceylon and Burma in search of fibres and grasses to be tested in his laboratory.

One weary day on October 21, 1879— after 13 months of repeated failures—he succeeded in his search for a filament that would stand the stress of electric current. This was how it happened:

Casually picking up a bit of lampblack, he mixed it with tar and rolled it into a thin thread. Then the thought occurred: why not try a carbonized cotton fiber? For 5 hours he work, but it broke before he could remove the mold. Two spools of thread were used up. At last a perfect strand emerged—only to be ruined when trying to place inside a glass tube. Edison refused to admit defeat. He continued

without sleep for two days and nights. Finally, he managed to slip one of the carbonized threads into a vacuum-sealed bulb. And he turned on the current. "The sight we had so long desired to see finally met our eyes."

His persistence amidst such discouraging odds has given the world the wonderful electric light!

394 Goodyear And Vulcanized Rubber

Charles Goodyear was repeatedly imprisoned for debt while developing his inventions, and perfected one while in jail. After years of patient toil, attended by visions of wealth, and the vicissitudes of poverty, he discovered the process of vulcanizing rubber. He could not convince any one outside of his family of the value of his discovery, and it was two years before he could secure the money to perfect his invention.

395 Epigram

●There aren't any hard-and-fast rules for getting ahead in the world—just hard ones.

●In order to live off a garden, you practically have to live in it.

—Kin Hubbard

●You don't have to lie awake nights to succeed. Just stay awake days.

—Healthways

●There is no poverty that can overtake diligence.　　　—Japanese Proverb

●By perseverance the snail reached the Ark.　　　　—Spurgeon

●Triumph is just umph added to try.

●It took me fifteen years to discover I had no talent for writing, but I couldn't give it up because by that time I was too famous.　　　—Robert Benchley

●When I was a young man I observed that nine out of ten things I did were failures. I didn't want to be a failure, so I

did ten times more work.
—George Bernard Shaw

PILGRIMAGE, LIFE

396 On His Way Home
A fugitive is one who is running from
home,
A vagabond is one who has no home;
A stranger is one away from home,
And a PILGRIM is on his way home.

397 Not Yet Home
I heard Dr. Morrison tell at Winona
Lake about his trip around the world,
preaching and teaching the gospel truth.
He went on this trip at the same time that
Roosevelt went to Africa. Morrison
preached the gospel at every port. "Teddy" went to Africa to do some exploring
and shoot a few water hogs. When he
came back, he was accorded a reception
such as few living men had. The governor
and the mayor greeted him, the bands
played, and countless thousands thronged
the wharf to welcome him.

Morrison came home. The governor of
the state did not come to meet him, nor
did the mayor or the police force. The fire
department never noticed him. No flags
were waving, no whistles blowing. He did
not even have a relative waiting for him.
In New York Roosevelt boarded a train
and had the same sort of reception all
over again when he reached his home
city. He was lauded and honored all the
way.

Morrison also boarded a train and
went home. He did not have a reception at
all. Nobody met him. The only person
who recognized him was the old baggage
master, and he just said, "Hello, there!" in
a casual sort of way.

Morrison said: "I picked up my heavy
grips and started off, all alone. I could not
help contrasting the homecoming of
Roosevelt with my own. God had privileged me to lead ten thousand souls to
Christ on that trip—and yet there I was,
without a soul to meet me! Nobody cared.
Suddenly I stopped. A new, glorious truth
had gripped me. And I found myself saying aloud, slowly, exultantly, 'Maybe I'm
not home yet! Maybe I'm not home!' "
—Words in Season

398 Homesick For Heaven
Homesick sometimes,
Want to go home;
Aching with longing
Where'er I roam.
Weary sometimes,
Wishing to be
There in the glory
Eternally.

Coming sometime,
Great trumpet sound!
Glorious daybreak!
Joy will abound.
Trading sometime
Body of clay,
For one immortal;
Hasten blest day!

—Lilian Guthrie

399 Nice Time Getting There
A skeptic once derided a Christian
man by asking him: "Say, George, what
would you say if when you die you found
there wasn't such a place as heaven after
all?"

With a smile the believer replied: "I
should say—well, I've had a fine time getting there anyway!"

Then the Christian sent a boomerang
back to the skeptic—a question not quite
so easy to answer.

"I say, Fred," he asked, "what would
you say if, when you die, *you found there
was such a place as hell after all?*"
—Free Methodist

117

PLEASURE

POLLUTION

400 More Money For Pleasure

By the end of 1912, nearly 50% of a worker's salary went for food. By the end of World War II, the household budget for food was 27%. By 1960, this portion had fallen to 22%. In 1976, it was down to 17%.

In early 1978, however, an upsurge was detected in cultivated home-cooking and in "luxury" foods. With increasing numbers of women at work in an affluent society, the nationwide annual food budget of Americans now total $215 billion.

401 Take Any Four Years

That prosperity and sensible spending do not go hand in hand is revealed by a glance at some statistics that were gleaned during a four-year period when the world was slowly climbing up out of the depression, and America went back into the pit of inebriation.

From 1932 to 1936 the income of the American people increased by 51 per cent. But during that same period they gave 30 per cent *less* to churches, 29 per cent *less* to benevolences, and 18 per cent *less* to colleges and other educational purposes. However, take a look at where a large percentage of this increase in income went. During that four-year period of increased earnings the people of the United States spent 48 per cent *more* for cigarettes and 317 per cent *more* for beer.

—*Evangelistic Illustration*

402 Epigram

●It now costs more to amuse a child than it once did to educate his father.

●Amusement is the happiness of those that cannot think.

—Alexander Pope

403 Polluting Air And Sea

Pollutants are the residues of things we used and throw away. The unfortunate thing is that as the earth becomes crowded, there is no longer any place to throw away anything and therefore the trash basket of the world becomes the air above or the sea below.

404 The Individual American

Meet the average American: "Every year he will leave in his wake his share of the 20 million tons of paper, 48 billion cans and 26 billion bottles that litter the land. He will personally pollute three million gallons of water in a year. He will pour enormous amounts of gases into the air from his car and other machines.

"Measured in terms of destructive effect on the environment, biologist Wayne David estimates that 1 American is equivalent to at least 25 citizens of India. Figuring in this way, 205 million Americans are now putting a drain on the resources of the earth that it would take 5 billion Indians to duplicate. And by the same reckoning, our population growth is far more dangerous to the survival of future generations than the much higher rate of China or Mexico."

405 Unusual Collection In Church

The collection—surely one of the most unusual ever taken in a church-stretched beyond the two pulpits, out two side doors, and down a corridor. The "take" weighed nearly a ton; it was inspired by a church-school class on ecology and a young women's adult study group.

The choir, in black and white robes, marched over and around stacks of bottles—whisky bottles and pop bottles and baby-food jars ... relish and rug cleaner, beer and beets . . . .

The Reverend Dwight S. Large, pastor of Detroit's Central Methodist Church, explained it all in his sermon: "We live in a moment of history when people choose death, poisoning the air and water with chemicals, and destroying the earth with sewage, pesticides, and trash. Each year we dump 28 billion bottles and 48 billion cans."

"More important," he continued, "action by every church and temple . . . might call attention to the fact that trash glass can be recycled and thus used and reused again and again." The bottles were destined for a collection station in Ann Arbor, then crushing, melting, and reuse.
— *Christianity Today*

POPULATION, EXPL.

406 The Doubling Population

It took from Creation to 1850 to reach 1 billion people. Since the population of the world in 1650 was an estimated 500 million, a doubling of world population took place in 200 years.

But it took only 80 years for the next doubling, as the population reached 2 billion around 1930.

In 1976, the population is over 4 billion—a doubling in 46 years. And it is estimated that the doubling rate is every 35 years.

407 Four Billion People Now

The world's population passed the four-billion mark in March 29, 1976, according to the population clock at the Museum of Science and Industry in Chicago. The museum officials said the mark was reached around midnight, Sunday, but nobody was around to see it and the night watchman evidently did not care.

The clock ticks away at the rate of about 2.2 persons a second, or about 190,000 a day. The rate is set by statistics

the museum receives periodically from the Population Reference Bureau, a private agency that collects data from every available source.

The world's population did not reach one billion until about 1850. The two-billion mark was reached in 1930 and the world grew to three billion in 1961.

408 A Continuous 2000-Story Building

If the present rate growth continues for 900 years, there will be some 60,000,000,-000,000,000 people on earth. This is 60 million billion people. Or 100 persons for each square inch of earth, including the land and sea.

Such a large number might be housed in a continuous 2,000-story building covering our entire planet—the upper 1,000 stories would simply contain the apparatus for running the gigantic unit. Half of the bottom 1,000 stories occupied by pipes, wires, and elevator shafts. This would leave 3 or 4 yards of floor space for each person.

409 Epigrams

●A father of 10 was asked why he had so many children. "Because," he said, "we never wanted the youngest one to be spoiled!"

●From the Des Moines *Register:* "She was reported in fair condition after giving birth to quintuplets Friday night. The father is a storkbroker."

●From a church notice in the York, Pa., Gazette and Daily: "Family Night—A Gift for the Largest Family Present. Sermon: 'Thou Fool.' "

●A book published in Bombay, India, entitled *Planned Families* contains the following publisher's warning: "Any reproduction strictly forbidden without our written permission."
— Noel Anthony

●Mark Cordell, manager of the Loveland, Colo., Chamber of Commerce, was attending a discussion of the population explosion when he was called home. His wife had just given birth to a boy. —UPI

PRAYER

410 Chained Together For 12 Centuries

St. Catherine's Monastery near Mt. Sinai, Egypt, has preserved the remains of three monks in accordance with their last requests made about 12 centuries ago. One was a doorkeeper who asked to hold his job forever and whose mummy has since been sitting beside the door he guarded in life. The other two monks took a vow, when young, to devote their lives to perpetual adoration, one praying while the other was asleep and vice versa.

Thereafter, they never saw nor spoke to each other again although they occupied adjoining cells. Their only connection was a chain, that ran through the wall and was fastened to their wrists, which each would tug as a signal when ready to begin and end his prayers. They died together and today their skeleton lie side by side in caskets and are still united by the same chain.

— Freling Foster

411 How Praying Hyde Prayed

Dr. Wilbur Chapman wrote to a friend: I have learned some great lessons concerning prayer. At one of our missions in England the audience was exceedingly small; but I received a note saying that an American missionary was going to pray for God's blessing down on our work. He was known as Praying Hyde. Almost instantly the tide turned. The hall became packed, and at my first invitation fifty men accepted Christ as their Saviour. As we were leaving I said, "Mr. Hyde, I want you to pray for me."

He came to my room, turned the key in the door, and dropped on his knees, and

waited five minutes without a single syllable coming from his lips. I could hear my own heart thumping, and his beating. I felt hot tears running down my face. I knew I was with God. Then, with upturned face, down while the tears were streaming, he said, "O God." Then for five minutes at least he was still again; and then, when he knew that he was talking with God there came from the depths of his heart such petitions for me as I had never heard before. I rose from my knees to know what real prayer was. We believe that prayer is mighty and we believe it as we never did before.

— Gospel Herald

412 Epigram

●Prayer is not overcoming God's reluctance, it is laying hold of His highest willingness.   — Archbishop Trench

●The only footprints on the sands of time, that will really last, are the ones made after knee-prints!
— C. W. Renwick

●Tennyson: More things are wrought by prayer than this world dreams of.

●Seven days without prayer makes one weak.   — The Bible Friend

●Groanings which cannot be uttered are often prayers which cannot be refused.   — C. H. Spurgeon

●Moody: "A man who prays much in private will make short prayers in public."

●When the outlook is bad, try the uplook!

●Martin Luther set apart his three best hours for prayer.

●George Muller said that the most important part of prayer was the fifteen minutes after he had said "Amen."

●Prayer gives you courage to make the decisions you must make in crisis and then the confidence to leave the result to a Higher Power.   — General Eisenhower

●The best prayers have often more groans than words.

413 Orville Mitchell's Urge To Stop

Probably everyone of us has at some time or another wondered how our prayers are being answered, but I recall one about which there is no doubt.

Once in the middle of the night I awoke in the most terrible moment of a very realistic dream. I was driving a car and I had just struck a child. The effect upon me was so real and terrible that I climbed out of bed, got down on my knees and asked my Father in heaven not to let that thing happen to me. Then it was as though the burden was taken from me, sleep was restored, and not another thought was given to the matter until noon next day.

Now five of us were in a car. I was at the wheel, and we were moving out Worth Street at around 25 miles per hour. Suddenly an urge to immediately stop came upon me with no apparent reason, and this we did quite abruptly.

When the other four passengers picked themselves off the dashboard and the back of the front seat, and all five of us tried to figure out why this abrupt stop was necessary, we were amazed to see a child dressed only in a diaper emerge between parked automobiles and waddle out into the street immediately in front of us.

Next a mother came charging out of the house, bounding over the curb and out into the street. She angrily grabbed up the child, and without much more than a glance in our direction retreated into the house.

To whom, do you suppose, has the Lord demonstrated his love in this remarkable answer to prayer? The little tot probably will never hear that his life was spared. The mother was so angry with herself for letting the child escape from the house that it is quite likely she never breathed one 'Thank You' to the Lord.

The other four occupants of the car, having heard the events leading up to the sudden stop, have asked me to tell the story on an occasion or two. But to me, who would have suffered most had the Lord not intervened, to me it has meant the most. All I can say in gratitude will confirm that the Psalmist was right when he said, "Whom have I in heaven but Thee, and there is none upon earth that I desire beside Thee."

—Orville Mitchell, Sr.

414 Rome's Thundering Legion

The two most famous legions in the Roman army were the Tenth Legion and the Thundering Legion. The Tenth Legion was composed of Caesar's veteran shock troops. In every great emergency it was upon that Legion that he called, and it never failed him. The Thundering Legion was the name given to the Militine Legion in the days of the philosopher emperor—and yet one of the worst persecutors of the Church—Marcus Aurelius.

Tertullian tells us how the legion won that name, the "Thundering Legion." In A.D. 176 the army of the emperor was engaged in a campaign against the Germans. In their march the Romans found themselves encircled by precipitous mountains which were occupied by their savage enemies. In addition to this danger the army was tormented by thirst because of the drought. It was then that the commander of the Praetorian Guard informed the emperor that the Militine Legion was made up of Christian, and that they believed in the power of prayer.

"Let them pray, then," said the emperor. The soldiers of the Legion then bowed on the ground and earnestly besought God in the name of Christ to deliver the Roman army. They had scarcely risen from their knees when a great thunderstorm arose, accompanied by hail. The storm drove the barbarians out of their strongholds; and, descending from the mountains, they entreated the

Romans for mercy. His army delivered from death at the hands of the barbarians, all delivered from death by the drought, the emperor decreed that this legion should be thereafter called the "Thundering Legion." He also abated somewhat his persecution of the Christians.

—C.E. Macartney

day of praying." Gen. Havelock rose at four, if the hour for marching was six, rather than lose the precious privilege of communion with God before setting out. Sir Matthew Hale says, "If I omit praying, and reading God's word, in the morning, nothing goes well all day."

—Foster

415 Allenby's Prayer For Jerusalem

Allenby Bridge was built to honor Allenby whom God used to miraculously make conquest of Jerusalem without the firing of a single gun. It spans the Jordan River.

Allenby told how as a little boy when he knelt to say his evening prayers he was taught to lisp after his mother the closing part of the prayer, "And, O Lord, we would not forget Thine ancient people, Israel; hasten the day when Israel shall again be Thy people and shall be restored to Thy favor and to their land."

At a reception in London, Allenby said, "I never knew then that God would give me the privilege of helping to answer my own childhood prayers."

—Chosen People

416 God Not In Junk Business

Dr. Walter Wilson and a missionary friend were praying for a car which was greatly needed for the missionary's work in Africa. The missionary prayed, "O God, You know how badly I need a car for my work. Do, Lord, send me a car. Any kind of an old, ramshackle car will do!" Dr. Wilson interrupted. "Stop praying that way, brother! God is not in the junk business!"

—Selected

417 Luther And Others On Devotions

Luther, when most pressed with his gigantic toils, said, "I have so much to do, that I cannot get on without three hours a

418 Baby's Earliest Memories

A caller found a young mother with her babe in her lap and her Bible in her hand. "Are you reading to your baby?" was the humorous query. "Yes," the young mother replied. "But, do you think he understands?" "I am sure he does not understand now, but I want his earliest memories to be that of hearing God's Word." God's Word is the "sword of the Spirit." Only by His Word are we purified and strengthened to do His will. It is impossible to overestimate the importance of reading the Word all through life.

—King's Business

419 Faraday's Escape To Prayer Meeting

A crowded gathering of distinguished scientists had been listening spellbound to the masterly expositions of Michael Faraday. For an hour he had held his brilliant audience enthralled as he demonstrated the nature and properties of the magnet. He had brought his lecture to a close with an experiment so novel, so bewildering, and so triumphant, that for some time after he resumed his seat, the house rocked with enthusiastic applause. And the the Prince of Wales—afterwards King Edward VII—rose to propose a motion of congratulation. The resolution, having been duly seconded, was carried with renewed thunders of applause.

Suddenly the uproar ceased and a strange silence settled over the audience. The assembly waited for Faraday's reply.

But he did not appear.

Only his most intimate friends knew

what had become of him. He was an elder in a little Sandemanian church—a church that never boasted more than twenty members.

The hour at which Faraday concluded his lecture was the hour of the weeknight prayer meeting.

—*Christus Medicus Magnus*

PREACHER

420 Longest Recorded Sermon

The longest sermon on record was preached by Rev. Robert Marshall, minister of the Birmingham Unitarian Church, Michigan, in 1976. He preached for 60 hours and 31 minutes. The previous record holder was Robert McKee who preached for 52 hours. He said that it took him two and a half years to write the 500,000-word sermon.

421 Shortest Sermon

When Roy DeLamotte was chaplain at Paine College in Georgia, he preached the shortest sermon in the college's history. However, he had a rather long topic. It was, "What Does Christ Answer When We Ask, 'Lord, What's in Religion for Me?' " The complete content of his sermon was one word: "Nothing." He explained later that the one-word sermon was meant for people "brought up on the 'gimme-gimme' gospel." When asked how long it took him to prepare the message, he said, "Twenty years."

—Ray O. Jones

422 Survey Of Sermons Preached In U.S.

In connection with my volumes of *Best Sermons*, I have sent invitations during the last 20 years to more than 120,000 clergymen who do preach. From the 15,000 to 22,500 sermon invitations issued for each volume, the average number of sermon manuscripts received for reading

and consideration has increased from 5,000 for the first volume to 6,000, 7,000, 7,500, and now nearly 8,000 per volume.

Ministers of 198 different denominations have been invited to submit sermons; men of 165 different denominations have responded with a total to date of more than 55,755 sermons. Sermons have been received in 15 different languages from ministers in 55 foreign countries.

About one minister in each thousand preaches in blank verse; one younger man preaches in blank verse every Sunday of the year!

Today, the better the sermon, the shorter it tends to be—18 to 20, 22, or 25 minutes. Generally speaking, the leading ministers and best preachers use more short illustrations rather than a few long stories. The best preaching is done in the great city churches of New York, Washington, Boston, Dallas, New Orleans, Miami, Los Angeles, Chicago.

A distinct difference marks most northern from southern preaching. In the South long illustrations—perhaps three or four—are customary in a sermon, while northern sermons may have 30 to 40 short, pithy allusions. Strong preachers are not limited to any specific locale, however, but may be found anywhere.

—*Christianity Today*

423 Some Popular Preachers

Henry Melvill is the most popular preacher in London. He prepares and preaches but one sermon in a week, which he always writes twice, very often three times.

Prof. Park, in his eloquent memoir of the late Mr. Homer, said: "The editor of Massilon's Lent Sermons regards it as a prodigy, that he finished a discourse in so short a time as ten or twelve days. This eminent preacher sometimes rewrote a single sermon fifteen or even twenty times. A distinguished scholar in our own land rewrote the most useful of his sermons thirteen or fourteen times, and labored, in connection with a literary friend, two whole days on as many sentences."

—W. Balkam

424 Why I Go To Church

Like most Laymen, I go to church to hear heralded the mind of Christ, not the mind of man. I want to hear expounded the timeless truth contained in the Scriptures, the kind of preaching that gets its power from "Thus saith the Lord." Such preaching is hard to find these days.

J. Howard Pew,
Board Chairman, Sun Oil Co.

425 Epigram

●The best preacher is the heart; the best teacher is time; the best book is the world; the best friend is God.

—The Talmud

●Great sermons begin in great hearts, and hearts are made great by tilling them with the needs of a brokenhearted, suffering world. Jesus' trained ears could hear a beggar's cry above the shouts of the throng.

●After his return from church one Sunday a small boy said, "You know what, Mommie? I'm going to be a minister when I grow up."

"That's fine," said his mother. "but what made you decide you want to be a preacher?"

"Well," said the boy pensively, "I'll have to go to church on Sunday anyway, and I think it would be more fun to stand up and yell than to sit still and listen.

—Sunshine Magazine

PREPAREDNESS

426 Preparing For Heaven, Anyone?

"Mamma," said a little child, "my Sunday-school teacher tells me that this world is only a place in which God lets us live a while, that we may prepare for a better world. But, Mother, I do not see anybody preparing. I see you preparing to go into the country, and Aunt Eliza is preparing to come here; but I do not see any one preparing to go there. Why don't they try to get ready?"

—Prairie Overcomer

427 King Insures Own Throne

The only King to insure himself against the loss of his throne was Prajadhipok, King of Siam from 1925 until he was forced to abdicate in 1935. Having taken out unemployment insurance policies with French and British underwriters early in his reign, Prajadhipok was able to live comfortably on the income from them until his death in 1941.

—Selected

428 The Fool Gave Him Back Staff

There was a certain nobleman who kept a fool, to whom he one day gave a staff, with a charge to keep it till he should meet with one who was a greater fool than himself. Not many years after, the nobleman was sick, unto death. The fool came to see him.

His sick lord said to him, "I must shortly leave you."—"And whither are you going," said the fool. —"Into another world," replied his lordship. "And when will you return? Within a month?"—"No"—"Within a year?"—"No."—"When, then?"—"Never!"—"Never?" said the fool.

"And what provision hast thou made for thy entertainment there, whither thou goest?"—"None at all."—"No!" said the fool; "none at all! Here, then take my staff; for, with all my folly, I am not guilty of any folly such as this."

—Bishop Hall

429 Epigram

● Chance favors only the mind which is prepared.

—Louis Pasteur

PROCRASTINATION

430 The Procrastinators Club Of America

"We're a little embarrassed," Les Waas, the president of the Procrastinators Club of America, announced recently in Philadelphia. "This is the first time we've observed National Procrastinators Week on time."

The Procrastinators Club, formed in 1957, is devoted to putting off just about everything until tomorrow—or even later. "We feel that anything worth doing is worth putting off," says Waas. None of the 80 or so members pay dues on time. "If they did, we'd throw them out.

"We feel that the ultimate thing to procrastinate against is war," he says. "Just think, if you keep putting off wars, eventually you might forget what you wanted to fight about."

—Selected

431 Cost Of "Wait A Minute"

Have you ever stopped to figure the cost of the phrase, "Wait a minute"? If you're making $5,000 a year, every minute you have to wait costs nearly 5 cents; at $10,000 a year this figure doubles to nearly 10 cents a minute. And, if you should reach the $100,000—a year category, your minutes will each be worth $1.

432 Epigrams

● Saying "It is too early," makes it too late. —Japanese Proverb

● Announcement by the Procrastination Club of America: "Last week was National Procrastination Week."

● One of the greatest labor saving devices of today is tomorrow.

● Alexander the Great, being asked how he had conquered the world, replied, "By not delaying." —Foster

● We cannot do everything at once, but we can do something at once.

—Calvin Coolidge

● It is never the wrong time to do the right thing. —Lutheran Digest

● A rolling stone gathers no moss.

—English Proverbs

● The best way to make your dreams come true is to wake up.

● Wisdom is knowing what to do next, skill is knowing how to do it, and virtue is doing it. —Everywoman's Family Circle

● Every time a man puts a new idea across, he finds ten men who thought of it before he did—but they only thought of it.

—Advertiser's Digest

● Young people tell what they are doing, old people what they have done and fools what they wish to do.

—French Proverb

—Better try to do something
  And fail in the deed
Than try to do nothing
  And always succeed.

—The Bible Friend

● Tomorrow's sale begins with today's service.

PURITY OF LIFE

433 Dannecker's New Desire

In his earlier life Dannecker, the sculptor, gained for himself a wonderful reputation for his statues of Ariadne and the Greek goddesses. Approaching his prime he felt he ought to devote all his strength and time to the creation of a masterpiece, so he set about to carve a figure of the Christ.

Twice he failed in his purpose, but finally he carved an image of Christ so perfect, so exquisitively beautiful that when people gazed upon it, they could only love and adore. Later Napoleon sent for him. "Come to Paris," he said, "and make for me a statue of Venus for the Louvre." But no such offer could tempt the heart of Dannecker. His reply was simple. "Sir, the hands that carved the Christ can never again carve a heathen goddess."

—*The Wind Blows*

434 Later Known As "Painter Of Peasants"

In his earlier years, Jean Francois Millet, the great French painter, devoted himself almost entirely to the painting of nude figures, according to the prevailing practice of the day. But one day, chancing to hear the lustful conversation of some men examining a picture of his in a window, he resolved to turn his talents in some other direction.

He and his wife were poor. It seemed to mean starvation to them both; but she consented, and he gave up nude art and began to paint peasant scenes. But what seemed to promise him only starvation brought him such fame as will doubtless prove immortal. He is known as "The Painter of Peasants," some of his most famous pictures being "The Sower," "The Gleaners," "The Shepherds," "Death and the Wood Cutter," and "The Angelus." This latter picture was once sold for $55,000, and is one of the art treasures of the world.

—*Current Anecdotes*

435 Epigram

●I believe in getting into hot water, I think it keeps you clean.

—G. K. Chesterton

R

RELIGIOSITY

436 Downward Trend

We remember hearing a leader of one of the great evangelical missionary societies commenting on what seems to be the natural development of many an organization. He said, there is a man. The man creates a movement or a mission. The mission gradually becomes a machine. Finally the machine ends up being a monument. Only the power of God can prevent a Christian organization from becoming a monument to the man who under God brought it into being.

—*Prairie Overcomer*

437 Hitler's Religiosity

Hitler knew how to dissemble. One had to look very closely at his terrible book Mein Kampf very carefully to see the cloven hoof beneath the angel's luminous robes.

He made free use of the Christian vocabulary, talked about the blessing of the Almighty and the Christian confessions which would become the pillars of the new state, he rang bells and pulled out all the organ stops. He assumed the earnestness of a man who is utterly weighed down by historic responsibility. He handed out pious stories to the press, especially the church papers.

It was reported, for example, that he showed his tattered Bible to some deaconesses and declared that he drew the strength for his great work from the Word of God. He was able to introduce a pietistic timbre into his voice which caused many religious people to welcome him as a man sent from God. And a skilled propaganda machine saw to it that despite all the atrocities which were already happening and despite the rabid invasions of the Nazis in the churches, the rumor got around that the good Fuhrer knew nothing about these things.

—Helmut Thielicke

438 Epigram

●Some folks think if they wear their best clothes on Sunday they're observing the Sabbath. —E.C. Mckenzie

REPENTANCE

439 Lincoln Proclaims National Fast Day

Abraham Lincoln wrote an address to the nation during the Civil War that was at least as important as the Gettysburg Address.

It was his proclamation for a national fast-day, by which he did designate and set apart Thursday the 30th day of April, 1863, as a day of national humiliation, fasting, and prayer.

Lincoln wrote: "It is the duty of nations as well as of men to own their dependence upon the overruling power of God; to confess their sins and transgressions in humble sorrow, yet with assured hope that genuine repentance will lead to mercy and pardon; and to recognize the sublime truth announced in the Holy Scriptures and proven by all history, that those nations only are blessed whose God is the Lord.

"The awful calamity of civil war which now desolates the land may be but a punishment inflicted upon us for our presumptuous sins, to the needful end of our national reformation as a whole people.

"Intoxicated with unbroken success, we have become too self-sufficient to feel the necessity too proud to pray to the God that made us.

"It behooves us, then, to humble ourselves before the offended Power, to confess our national sins, and to pray for clemency and forgiveness."
— *The Bible Friend*

440 Satan Told Him To Pray

There is an Eastern story of a Sultan who overslept himself, so as not to awaken at the hour of prayer. So the Devil came and waked him, and told him to get up and pray.

"Who are you?" said the Sultan. "Oh, no matter," replied the other. "My act is good, is it not? No matter who does the good action, so long as it is good."

"Yes," replied the Sultan; "but I think you are Satan. I know your face; you have some bad motive." "But," says the other, "I am not so bad as I am painted. You see I have left off my horns and tail. I am pretty good fellow, after all. I was an angel once, and still keep some of my original goodness." "That's all very well," replied the sagacious and prudent caliph, "but you are the tempter; that's your business; and I wish to know why you want me to get up and pray."

"Well," said the Devil with a flirt of impatience, "if you must know, I will tell you. If you had slept and forgotten your prayers, you would have been sorry for it afterward, and penitent; but if you go on as now, and do not neglect a single prayer for ten years, you will be so satisfied with yourself that it will be worse for you than if you had missed one sometimes and repented of it. God loves your fault mixed with penitence more than your virtue seasoned with pride."
— Walter Baxendale

441 Epigram

● No man is rich enough to buy back his past.   — Oscar Wilde

● True repentance has a double aspect; it looks upon things past with a weeping eye, and upon the future with a watchful eye.   — Robert Smith

● There is a tradition that the lily sprang from the repentant tears of Eve as she went forth from Paradise.

RESURRECTION

442 Lady's Eternal Burial Place?

A certain Hanoverian countess, who lived about a hundred years ago, was a noted unbeliever, and was especially opposed to the doctrine of the resurrection, as indeed every unbeliever might well be, especially if his opposition could alter it.

This lady died when about thirty years of age. Before her death she gave orders that her grave should be covered with a slab of granite; that around it should be placed square blocks of stone, and that the corners should be fastened to each other and to the granite slab by heavy iron clamps.

Upon the covering this inscription was placed:

THIS BURIAL PLACE
PURCHASED TO ALL ETERNITY
MUST NEVER BE OPENED

All that human power could do to prevent any change in that grave was done. But a little birch tree seed sprouted, and the root found its way between the side stone and the upper slab and grew there. Slowly but steadily it forced its way until the iron clamps were torn asunder, the granite lid was raised, and it is now resting upon the trunk of the birch tree, which is large and flourishing.

—Selected

443 A Tree Out Of Her Grave

In Tewin churchyard, a short distance from King's Cross Station, in England, stands a great four-trunked tree growing out of a grave. Its presence there has given rise to much speculation among the residents of that section. The grave from which it grows is that of Lady Anne Grimston.

Is the tree a monument to a woman's disbelief or did it happen to grow there merely by chance? Nobody knows.

Lady Anne Grimston did not believe in life after death. When she lay dying in her palatial home, she said to a friend, "I shall live again as surely as a tree will grow from my body."

She was buried in a marble tomb. The grave was marked by a large marble slab, and surrounded by an iron railing. Years later the marble slab was found to be moved a little. Then it cracked, and

through the crack a small tree grew.

The tree continued to grow, tilting the stone and breaking the marble masonry until today it has surrounded the tomb with its roots, and has torn the railing out of the ground with its massive trunks. The tree at Lady Anne Grimston's grave is one of the largest in England.

Was it mere chance that caused the tree to grow there? Perhaps God the Almighty took her challenge.

—Pastor's Manual

444 The 11,111 Heads

According to Dr. E. R. Bull, a Methodist missionary to the Ryuku Islands of Japan, a huge grave has been discovered on the Island of Amakusa, where a marker states that the heads of 11,111 Christians are buried there. The date of the grave is 1637, in which year the Japanese government ordered all Christians exterminated, and the inscription above this grave states that 11,111 Christians were killed, and that their bodies were buried separately.

The purpose in this was that the missionaries who had brought Christianity to Japan had preached the resurrection of the body, and the Japanese rulers supposes that separating the heads from the rest of the bodies in burial, there could be no possibility of the Christians coming forth from their graves.

—Selected

445 The 800-Year Rose

In Romsey, England, an expert in ancient plants has identified a seed discovered inside an abbey wall as an 856-year-old rose. Workmen found the rose behind a medieval painting in a hole sealed in 1120.

Think of it! A seed preserved and isolated for 856 years. That seed which was never allowed to fall into the ground, die, and spring up as a beautiful rose bush.

—Prairie Overcomer

REVIVAL

446 Religious America

In the USA, at the declaration of independence, only 5% were Christians. By the Civil War, the figure rose to 12%. At the turn of the century, 1/4 of the people included Christians.

Billy Graham told reporters in 1977 that 40% of Americans claim they have been born again, and 95% of young people believed in a personal God.

447 Subractions Also

When I talk about blessing I not only mean additions, but subtractions, too. A pastor came to one of his fellow pastors and said, "We've had a revival in our church." The other man replied, "That's good. How many were added to your church?" "None were added, but ten were subtracted." That's spiritual prosperity. It may mean subtraction. If some of our churches had the unconverted deacons subtracted, revival would come.

—*Moody Monthly*

448 Dividing Line On Prairies

I remember when as a young Christian worker I held an evangelistic campaign in a church at a crossroad, way out on the prairie. It was just a little church. There was a center aisle, and the seats went over against the wall from that aisle. We had very good congregations, but nothing else. After several nights of trying to preach, and giving an invitation, the pastor said to me:

"Years ago a family in this church quarreled, and the community has taken sides in the matter. The members of the family do not speak to each other and that aisle down the center of the church divides the factions. The people on the one side will not speak to those on the other."

One night I don't know what hap-pened, but when the meeting ended, the two who had a grievance against each other met in front of the pulpit, asking each other for forgiveness. Then the thing broke loose. There were just two nights left. The night we closed the campaign, the pastor stood with me on the doorstep of that little church. He said, "Look out there over the prairie"—and all who have been on the prairies of Nebraska know that you can see for miles. "I don't believe there is a single unsaved man left in any farmhouse in sight."

God gathered them all during the last two or three nights, when the Christians got right with each other and with God.

—Will M. Houghton

449 Epigram

●John Wesley: "Give me one hundred men who fear nothing but sin, and desire nothing but God, and I will shake the world."

ROMAN CATHOLICISM

450 Roman Catholic Statistics

The Roman Catholic Church has an estimated 665,000,000 members, or about 18% of the world's population. In the United States, there were 48.8 million Catholics in 1976, or 22% of the US population.

In addition, the Pope commands well over a million ecclesiastics—425,000 priests and 900,000 nuns. There are 4,000 cardinals, patriarchs, metropolitans, archbishops, bishops, abbots and superiors.

Churches number 420,000.

451 Wealth Of Vatican

Not only is the Roman Catholic Church the largest religious organization in the world, it is the richest. The securities alone which it holds are conservatively estimated at $6 billion, making it by far the largest single stockholder in the world.

It is virtually impossible to estimate its wealth in ancient buildings and art treasures, which would have to be in the billions of dollars.

Moreover, the Vatican continues to be one of the world's greatest hoarders of gold. According to Stefan Jean Rundt, head of S. J. Rundt and Association, the Vatican has a standing order to buy a half million ounces of gold every two weeks. The Vatican reportedly has a gold reserve three times that of Great Britain.

452 First Survey Of Paradise

Vatican City (Reuter)—Heaven has more Italian saints in it than any other nationality, according to an unofficial Vatican study.

The survey, carried out by Dutch Jesuit Rene Mols, shows that of 1,848 registered saints, 626 are Italians, informed sources said.

Further breakdown of what has been termed 'official Paradise,' shows that more than half (1,044) of Heaven's Catholic saints were priests during their time on earth.

But their number also include 15 ex-Popes, 14 former married women and eight widowers.

The nation with the second highest number of saints is France (576), followed by the British Isles (271) and the Iberian peninsula (215).

The study was made of all saints cannonized in the past 1,000 years and may form the basis of a demographic survey of Paradise to be carried out by the Vatican computer, the sources said.

The computer, housed in the Vatican's Central Statistics Office, recently calculated that the proportion of Catholics in the world population fell between 1970 and 1971 from 18.4 percent to 18.2 percent.

At the last count, 664,388,000 of the world's 3,645,829,000 inhabitants were Catholics, the computer estimated.

S

SACRIFICE

453 God Counted Crosses
I counted dollars while God counted
    crosses,
I counted gains while He counted
    losses,
I counted by worth by the things
    gained in store
But He sized me up by the scars that I
    bore.
I coveted honors and sought for
    degrees,
He wept as He counted the hours on
    my knees;
I never knew until one day by the
    grave
How gain are the things that we spend
    life to save;
I did not yet know until my loved one
    went above
That richest is he who is rich in God's
    love.

— The Brethren Evangelist

454 Whither Goest Thou?
During the first persecution of Christians by Emperor Nero, Christians begged
Peter not to expose his life which was
considered necessary to the well-being of
the church. Finally, Peter consented to
depart from Rome, but as he fled along the
Appian Way, about two miles from the
gates, he was met by a vision of the
Saviour travelling towards the city.

Struck with amazement, he exclaimed,
"Lord, whither goest thou?" The Saviour,
looking upon him with a mild sadness,
replied, "I go to Rome to be crucified a
second time," and vanished. Peter
immediately turned back and reentered
the city.

— Jameson

455 "We Already Died"
When James Calvert went out to can-
nibal Fiji with the message of the Gospel,
the captain of the ship in which he traveled sought to dissuade him. "You will
risk your life and all those with you if you
go among such savages," he said. Calvert's
magnificent reply was, "We died before
we came here." And yet he would have
been the last to talk about a sacrifice; it
was not a life of sacrifice, but of real
pleasure.

— King's Business

456 Epigram

●Jim Elliot, martyr: "He is no fool who gives what he cannot keep, to gain what he cannot lose."

●There has never yet been a man in our history who led a life of ease whose name is worth remembering.

— Theodore Roosevelt

●The wise man does not expose himself needlessly to danger, since there are few things for which he cares sufficiently; but he is willing, in great crises, to give even his life — knowing that under certain conditions it is not worthwhile to live.

— Aristotle

SALVATION

457 Peace Child

In a book entitled *Peace Child*, Don Richardson records the moving account of how the Sawi people of Irian Jaya came to understand salvation through Jesus Christ. For many months he and his family sought for some way to communicate the gospel to this tribe. Then they discovered the key for which they had been praying. All demonstrations of kindness expressed by the Sawi were regarded with suspicion except one act. If a father gave his own son to his enemy, his sacrificial deed showed that he could be trusted! Furthermore, everyone who touched that child was brought into a friendly relationship with the father. The Sawi were then taught that in a similar way God's beloved Son could bring them eternal peace.

— *Our Daily Bread*

458 The Twice-Saved Churchill

A wealthy family in England, took their children to the country. The children went swimming in a pool. One of the boys began to drown. The son of the gardener jumped in and rescued the helpless one. The grateful parents asked the gardener what they could do for the youthful hero. The gardener said his son wanted to go to college — "He wants to be a doctor." "We'll be glad to pay his way through," they told him.

When Winston Churchill was striken with pneumonia after the Teheran Conference, the King of England instructed that the best doctor be found to save the Prime Minister. The doctor was Mr. Fleming, the developer of penicillin. "Rarely," said Churchill to Fleming, "has one man owed his life twice to the same rescuer." It was Fleming who saved Churchill in that pool.

459 Engineer's Son At Apex

Pliny relates a story of the setting up of an obelisk. The stone was to stand ninety-nine feet in height; 20,000 workmen were to pull at the rope and to work the hoisting apparatus. There was great responsibility and risk in the operation. The king resorted to a singular expedient to insure the best attention and skill from the engineer. He ordered the engineer's own son to be bound to the apex, so that his heart as well as his head should be under the sternest tension.

The kingdom of Christ in our homes and in our churches is the great spiritual erection of our times. Our own sons are bound to the obelisk; our children will share the fate controlled by our fidelity. We cannot escape this fearful issue.

— F.E. Clark

460 Epigram

●Oh, that someone would arise, man or god, to show us God. — Socrates

●A boy was in danger of being drowned while bathing in a river. Seeing a traveller on the bank, he called to him for help; but the man started to lecture him on his rashness. "Rescue me now," cried the boy; "you can lecture me later on when I am safe." — Fable of Aesop

SALVATION, ASSURANCE

461 God Would Be Greater Loser

The old Scotch lady was right. When she was visited by a very young minister who was short on experience, she held fast to her firm assurance of her safety in Christ. "But just suppose that after all God should let you sink into hell?" said the minister. "He would lose more than I would," came the firm answer to faith. "All I would lose would be my own soul, but He would lose His good name."

—Donald Grey Barnhouse

462 "Whom Are You Doubting?"

I often use this illustration told by J. Wilbur Chapman, to close the message:

I will tell you how to be saved, and how you may know you are a Christian. I was studying for the ministry, and I heard that D.L. Moody was to preach in Chicago, and I went down to hear him. I finally got into him after the meeting, and I shall never forget the thrill that went through me, when he came and sat down beside me, an inquirer. He asked me if I was a Christian. I said, "Mr. Moody, I am not sure whether I am a Christian or not."

He asked whether I was a church member, and I said I was, but was not always sure whether I was a Christian or not. He very kindly took his Bible and opened it at the fifth chapter of John, the twenty-fourth verse, which read as follows: "Verily, verily, I say unto you, He that heareth my word and believeth on him that sent me *hath* everlasting life and shall not come into condemnation; but is passed from death unto life.

Suppose you had read that for the first time, wouldn't you think it was wonderful? I read it through, and he said: "Do you believe it?" I said, "Yes." "Do you accept it?" I said, "Yes." "Well, are you a Christian?" "Mr. Moody, I sometimes think I am, and sometimes I am afraid I am not."

He very kindly said, "Read it again."

So I read it again, "Verily, verily, I say unto you, He that heareth my word and believeth on him that sent me hath everlasting life, and shall not come into condemnation, but *is passed* from death unto life."

Then he said, "Do you believe it?" I said, "Yes." "Do you receive *Him?*" I said, "Yes." "Well" he said, "are you a Christian?"

I just started to say over again that sometimes I was afraid I was not, when, the only time in all the years I knew him and loved him, he was sharp with me. He turned on me with his eyes flashing and said, "See here, whom are you doubting?"

Then I saw it for the first time, that when I was afraid I was not a Christian I was doubting God's Word. I read it again with my eyes overflowing with tears.

Since that day I have had many sorrows and many joys, but never have I doubted for a moment that I was a Christian, because God said it.

Now what I ask you to do is to plant your feet upon this promise, and say, "Yes, from this moment I know I am a Christian.

—Carl Johnson

SALVATION-"NOT BY WORKS"

463 Everything For Nothing

An aged saint, on being asked to describe salvation, aptly replied, "Something for nothing." Another aged saint, who had weathered the storms for many a long year and was nearing the Heavenly harbor, on hearing this story related, exclaimed, "Yes, it's even better than that. It's everything for nothing."

—Grace Robinson

464 Only Two Religions

While presenting the Gospel on the street of a California city, we were often interrupted about as follows: "Look here, sir! There are hundreds of religions in this country, and the followers of each sect think theirs the only right one. How can poor plain men like us find out what really is the truth?" We generally replied something like this: "Hundreds of religions, you say? That's strange; I've heard of only two." "Oh, but you surely know there are more than that?"

"Not at all, sir. I find, I admit, many shades of difference in the opinions of those comprising the two great schools; but after all there are but two. The one covers all who expect salvation by doing; the other, all who have been saved by something done. So you see the whole question is very simple. Can you save yourself, or must you be saved by another? If you can be your own savior, you do not need my message. If you can not, you may well listen to it."

—H. A. Ironside

465 The Key . . . After 29 Floors

Three men, John Newton, Louis Weatherford, and Samuel Preston, were out to find the best that this life had to offer. Willing to try anything, they were now on their way to New York City to "paint the town red." With a whole week ahead of them, they were anticipating some high times. They had money, position and culture. The only thing they wanted was action and they were now ready to get it.

As the "Silver Star" glided to a stop at Grand Central, three men, full of excitment and frivolity, stepped off the train into a busy world. Amidst the confusion the three jovial men were able to hail a cab and direct the driver to the Ambassador Hotel where they wanted to board. The cabby promptly took them to their destination, received his tip and disappeared into the throng of cars. As the cab drove off, the three men just stood on the pavement staring up the side of this twenty-nine floor building. They were

amazed at the sight of such a tall structure.

Upon entering the hotel, they were greeted by a bellhop who took their bags and led them to the main desk. At the desk the clerk asked them what type of room they wanted and the three men replied, "Give us the best you have!" The clerk looked at the register and then told the men that the only one of this type left was on the top floor. It had a TV, two cushioned chairs, four beds with innermen said a few words to each other and quickly decided to take it. The key was handed over and the bellhop led them to the elevator.

After arranging their belongings in the proper order, the three men put on their tweed suits, left the key at the desk and were off to see New York City's high spots. Hours went by and the three began to get weary so they headed back to the hotel. At the lobby desk they were told the elevator had developed some complications and was not able to take them upstairs. They were given the alternative of either walking up twenty-nine flights of steps or sleeping in a small, less luxurious room on the second floor. The three huddled together and decided to take the long walk upstairs and enjoy the comforts of their own room, so up they started.

The first few flights went quickly and easily and the three companions were joking and having a good time. Each flight seemed a little bit longer but the men kept pressing on. Five, six, seven floors were passed and each one meant that they were one flight closer to the top. The men, already weary from a hard night, began to slow down and the floors dragged by slower each time. Eleventh, twelfth, thirteenth floor was passed, "Almost halfway there," said Louis. The other just grunted and they pushed on. Seventeen, eighteen . . . . they wondered if they would ever reach the top. On the twentieth floor Sam sat down and said he couldn't go on.

After resting a few moments the others finally persuaded him to try it .... after all only nine floors left and then those nice, soft mattresses, and fried chicken and ...., so on they went.

Each flight seemed like a mile and it seemed as if it took an eternity to get there. All three men were now on their knees, crawling step by step in hopes of reaching the twenty-ninth floor. Just one more to go. Slowly they proceeded, inch by inch until John shouted out that he could see the room, only eight more steps and then about fifteen feet down the hall. With his added inspiration each fellow put all the energy into it that he had and to their relief they were all on the last floor. They had reached their goal now, as soon as the door would be opened, they would enjoy all the luxuries which had spurred them on during their climb.

Sam was the first to come to the door so he reached down into his pocket for the key. To Sam's amazement the key wasn't there. He asked John if he had it but John said that Louis must have it. They both looked at Louis but all he had was several empty pockets. Here they were on the twenty-ninth floor just inches from what they considered 'Heaven' and yet they could not get in. They had forgotten to get the key.

The Bible Friend.

SALVATION—"WHOSOEVER"

466 Ol' Man Kline

A certain Mr. Kline, discouraged, defeated, and convinced that life just wasn't worth living because no one cared for him, walked past a church one Sunday evening when services were in progress. As the congregation sang he caught the strains of that familiar hymn: "Saved by grace alone, this is all my plea. Jesus died for all mankind, and Jesus died for me."

His hearing, however, was not very good, so when the congregation came to the words, "Jesus died for all mankind," he thought they sang, "Jesus died for ol' man Kline." "Why", he said, "that's me!" Stopping in his tracks, he turned and entered the small auditorium. There he heard the simple message of the Gospel as the minister presented the good news that Jesus Christ came into the world to save sinners. Mr. Kline believed and was saved.

—Richard De Haan

467 The Word "Whosoever"

I thank God for that word "whosoever." If God had said there was mercy for Richard Baxter, I am so vile a sinner, that I would have thought he meant some other Richard Baxter; but, when he says whosoever, I know that includes me, the worst of all Richard Baxters.

—Baxter

468 Many Not Any

Lady Huntington was a Christian well known to others during the time of the revival that swept England in the nineteenth century. She was once asked how she, one of the country's noblewomen, had been converted. She replied: "By one letter."

"How is that? By one letter?"

"Yes," she answered, "In God's Word, I Corinthians 1:26, it says: 'Not many noble are called. That 'm' saved my soul; for if He had said, 'Not any noble,' I must have been damned. So God blessed the little letter 'm' before any to the salvation of my soul."

—Al Bryant

SECOND COMING

469 Repeated Promises Of Coming

Both the Old and New Testaments are filled with promises of the Second Coming of Christ. There are 1,845 references to it in the Old Testament, and a total of seventeen Old Testament books give it prominence.

Of the 216 chapters in the entire New Testament, there are 318 references to the Second Coming, or one out of 30 verses. Twenty-three of the 27 New Testament books refer to this great event. The four missing books include three which are single-chapter letters written to individual persons on a particular subject, and the fourth is Galatians which does imply Christ's coming again.

For every prophecy on the First Coming of Christ, there are 8 on Christ's Second Coming.

470 Exobiology

A brand-new science called "Exobiology" came into being in the 1960's. This science is dedicated specifically to the study of extra-terrestrial life. In laboratories, at giant radio observatories and at esoteric symposiums, some of the world's keenest intellects are focusing on this new discipline. Someone, however, has sardonically called exobiology a science "that has yet to demonstrate that its subject matter exists."

It *will* be demonstrated at the sudden coming of Christ.

471 Signs In The Sky

In Bombay, India, 100 girls from a missionary home were holding a Christian service on the street one evening when they all saw in the sky an immense semicircle of letters of fire, which read: "JESUS IS COMING SOON."

Then, in Sweden, 300 people were returning from an all-night prayer meeting. Suddenly they saw a hand pointing to words which were written in large letters in the heavens: "SEE, I COME QUICK-LY."

In York, Pennsylvania, Dr. H. E. Kline called out on a case at 2 AM., noticed an abnormally brilliant star. Some distance

from it he saw a distinct cross with a silvery sheen on one side and a crimson glow on the other. Above was a diadem, a crown of stars. Dr. Kline called his family and they watched this amazing sight until it disappeared at 4 AM.

—Charles E. Taylor in
Jesus is Coming

472 Mrs. Tan's Vision Of Cross

The New Grace Christian Church in the Philippines has a distinctively massive Cross outside its sanctuary.

One mid-morning in 1976, Mrs. Julia L. Tan was returning home from a God-honoring project in Manila when she saw a beautiful, shining Cross over the church's existing cross structure. Disbelieving her own eyes, she thought it must be a case of "double vision."

The shining Cross disappeared. But in another minute, the Cross again appeared over the roof of the church. This precious experience proved a great comfort and assurance to her in the ministry.

Mrs. Tan co-founded the 4,500-student Grace Christian High School and Grace Bible Church, and started the Grace Gospel Church and Grace Christian Church. She still actively serves the Lord, having completed 50 years of educational service in the Far East by 1977.

473 Horses' Long Wait For Rider

The most remarkable horse in the world has been kept in readiness since 1072 for the expected resurrection of Sultan Muhammad Ibn Daud. The sultan ruled Iran as well as a large contiguous territory between the Tigris and the Oxus and his reign has been termed Iran's Golden Age. He extended the frontiers of his country through conquest and expansion, accumulating great wealth in the process.

As soon as he died and was laid to rest, myth and legend seized upon his memory, embroidering it with prophecies derived from national yearnings. It was said that he would rise from his tomb, mount his horse and lead his subjects to new conquests and glory. So strong was this belief that in all the intervening centuries a thoroughbred charger—complete with saddle and groom—has been kept in readiness before his tomb in the Mosque of Kuchan, province of Khorasan, waiting for the day when the dead sultan will emerge from his tomb to resume the reins of both mount and government. It is one of the strangest manifestations of enduring faith and loyalty to be found in the modern world.

—Selected

SELF-CENTEREDNESS

474 License Plate No. 1

Paul Powell, Illinois secretary of state, had to decide who would get auto license plate No. 1. "It was a real problem," he said. "I'm not about to assign it to someone and make about a thousand other people feel hurt." His solution? He assigned it to himself.

—Gospel Herald

475 "Just You And Me"

Dear Friend:

Our church membership	
Nonresident membership	75
Balance left to do the work	1325
Elderly folks who have done their share in the past	25
Balance left to do the work	1300
Sick and shut-in folks	25
Balance left to do the work	1275
Membership who did not pledge	350
Christmas and Easter members	300
Balance left to do the work	625
Members who are too tired and overworked	300
Balance left to do the work	325
Alibiers	200
Balance left to do the work	125
Members who are too busy somewhere else	123
Balance left to do the work	2

Just you and me—and brother, you'd better get busy, for it's too much for me!

—Progress

476 Pink Was Empress' Property

The Russian empires Elizabeth Petrovna, daughter of Peter the Great, had a strange liking for the shade of pink. She was so jealous of this tint that she issued a decree making it a capital crime for any other woman in her empire to wear a pink garment—visible or concealed. The empress prided herself on being an opponent of capital punishment. But any woman caught in a violation of the pink law was liable to mutilation or deportation to Siberia—or both.

477 Epigram

●"Be Yourself!" is about the worse advice you can give to some people.

●My idea of an agreeable person is one who agrees with me.

—Samuel Johnson

●Admiration: Our polite recognition of another person's resemblance to ourselves.

●Some people have a keen sense of humor. The more you humor them, the better they like it.

●You can always tell when a man's well-informed. His views are pretty much like your own.   —Louie Morris

●For an impenetrable shield, stand inside yourself.   —Thoreau

●Most people enjoy the inferiority of their best friends.   —Lord Chesterfield

●He that falls in love with himself will have no rivals.   —Franklin

●Talk to a man about himself and he

will listen for hours.   —Disraeli

● He who thinks himself good for everything is often good for nothing.
          —Picard

● The smallest package we have ever seen is a man wrapped up in himself.

● The husband who boasts that he never made a mistake has a wife who did.

● In the post office of a prideful small town in New York State, appropriate signs were posted over the outgoing-mail slots. One sign read "Webster," the town's name; the other read "Rest of the World."

SEPARATION, WORLDLY

478 Robinson Wanted Not A Thing

Bud Robinson, the well-known Holiness preacher, was taken by friends to New York and shown around the city. That night in his prayers he said, "Lord, I thank You for letting me see all the sights of New York. And I thank You most of all that I didn't see a thing that I wanted!"

Blessed is the man who can sit loose to the charms of this old world, independent of them because he doesn't want them.

479 Unless It Got Inside

All the water in the world,
    However hard it tried,
Could never sink a ship
    Unless it got inside.

All the evil in the world,
    The wickedness and sin,
Can never sink the soul's craft
    Unless it got inside.
          —Selected

480 Marching Off The World

Harold Lamb's *Life of Alexander the Great* .... describes memorably the consternation which came upon the Greek army following Alexander across Asia Minor, when they discovered that they had marched clear off the map. The only maps they had were Greek maps, showing only a part of Asia Minor. The rest was blank space.

Isn't this what Christians are to do?

481 Epigram

● If it's really true that "all the world is a stage," then God's children should all have stage-fright.   — *The Bible Friend*

● John Newton's life rule: "I make it a rule of Christian duty never to go to a place where there is not room for my Master as well as myself."

● The eagle that sears in the upper air does not worry itself about crossing rivers.   — *Calendar*

SIN

482 What Is Sin

Man calls it an *accident*; God calls it an *abomination*.

Man calls it a *blunder*; God calls it a *disease*.

Man calls it a defect; God calls it a disease.

Man calls it a *chance*; God calls it a *choice*.

Man calls it an *error*; God calls it an *enmity*.

Man calls it a *fascination*; God calls it a *fatality*.

Man calls it an *infirmity*; God calls it an *iniquity*.

Man calls it a *luxury*; God calls it a *leprosy*.

Man calls it a *liberty*; God calls it *lawlessness*.

Man calls it a *trifle*; God calls it a *tragedy*.

Man calls it a mistake; God calls it a *madness*.

Man calls it a *weakness*; God calls it *willfulness*.

          — *Moody Monthly*

139

483 When God Blushed

An old Welsh poem tells how the Creator once held a review of the heavenly bodies. One by one, sun, moon, stars, and all the host of heaven passed by, and as they passed by, their august Maker greeted them with a smile. But when the earth passed, God blushed!

Yes, it matters not how fair the beginning of life, or how unclouded its early sky, every man comes at length within that shadow which is as eternal as human history, the deep, deep shadow of sin.

—C.E. Macartney

484 "All Is Discovered"

There is a tradition to the effect that Noel Coward sent identical notes to twenty most prominent men in London, saying, "All is discovered. Escape while you can."

All twenty abruptly left the town.

485 "I'm A Good Sinner"

I have met a few people who have tried to convince me that they were not bad sinners. I met such a lady in Bluefield, West Virginia. This well-dressed woman came forward on the salvation invitation. I took her hand and prepared to give her a prayer to repeat after me. The prayer I usually give is, "Dear Lord, I know that I am a no-good sinner. I know I can't save myself. I do need forgiveness for my awful sins. I can't do without you, Jesus. Please forgive me for my many sins. I here and now receive You into my heart as my personal Saviour. I'll try to live for You from this night on. I pray my prayer in Jesus' Name. Amen!" Thousands of people seeking to be saved have prayed this prayer with me.

I took this woman's hand and began to give her the prayer to repeat after me. "Dear Lord, I know I'm a no-good sinner." She never said a word. I looked at her and said, "Don't you want to be saved?"

She said, "Yes, Eddie, I do want to be saved, but I'm not a sinner."

"Then you can't be saved," I said, "Jesus only died for sinners."

"But, Mr. Martin," she replied, "I'm a good sinner."

"A good sinner! Lady, there are no good sinners. You will have to take your seat. God can't save you until you become conscious that you are a no-good sinner and need His forgiveness."

"But, Mr. Martin, you don't understand. I'm really not a bad sinner."

I told her to go back and sit down. She held on to my hand with a vise-like grip. Finally she looked me in the eyes and said, "Oh, please forgive me. I know I am a no-good hell-deserving sinner. I am a proud, no-good sinner. I do need Christ to forgive me of my sins."

"Wonderful! Now, lady, you are ready to do business with God." We prayed together there at the front, thousands of people looking on. The lady came clean with God. God saved her. But she never would have been saved if she had not changed her attitude. None of us are good sinners. We are all big sinners, bad sinners.

—Eddie Martin

SMALL THINGS

486 Those Little Hurts

Termites destroy more property than do earthquakes. More fires are caused by matches and cigarettes than by volcanoes.

More heartaches and sorrow are caused by little words and deeds of unkindness than by open acts of dislike and enmity.

487 From Kimball To Graham

A Sunday School teacher, a Mr. Kimball, in 1858 led a Boston shoe clerk to give his life to Christ. The clerk, Dwight L. Moody, became an evangelist and in

England in 1879 awakened evangelistic zeal in the heart of Frederick B. Meyer, pastor of a small church.

F. B. Meyer, preaching on an American college campus, brought to Christ a student named J. Wilbur Chapman. Chapman engaged in YMCA work employed a former baseball player Billy Sunday, to do evangelistic work.

Sunday held a revival in Charlotte, North Carolina. A group of local men were so enthusiastic afterward that they planned another campaign, bringing Mordecai Hamm to town to preach.

In the revival, a young man named Billy Graham heard the gospel and yielded his life to Christ.

Billy Graham . . . (The story goes on and on).

488 How Chicago Fire Started

Many years ago, in 1871 in Chicago a woman was milking her cow, and there was a little lamp of oil, a little flickering flame. The cow kicked over the lamp, and the flame kindled a wisp of hay, and another wisp, until all the hay in the stable was on fire, and the next building was on fire, and the next and the next!

The fire spread over the river to the main part of Chicago and swept on until, within a territory one mile wide and three miles long, there were only two buildings standing. The little flame from that lamp had laid Chicago in ashes!

—R. A. Torrey

489 Epigram

●A sparrow is small; still, it's a bird.
—Russian Proverb

●Big shots are small shots who keep on shooting.

●For want of a nail the shoe was lost; for want of a shoe the horse was lost; and for want of a horse the rider was lost; being overtaken and slain by the enemy, all for the want of care about a horseshoe nail.   —Benjamin Franklin

SOUL WINNING

490 The 95% Estimate

It has been estimated that probably 95% of all church members have never led anyone to Christ.

491 Billy Graham's Total Attendances

Evangelist Billy Graham and his associates preached to 53,561,970 people at crusades and rallies from 1947 to 1977, according to Billy Graham Evangelistic Association staff.

There were 1,626,886 inquirers who recorded decisions at the crusades and rallies during the same period.

The total does not reflect the thousands of decisions made by persons hearing and seeing Graham on radio and television. They also do not include single meetings Mr. Graham addressed during the two years of his crusades in 1947-1949.
—Information supplied
through Mr. Roque Tan

492 Epigram

●Go for souls, and go for the worst.

SPEED

493 Progressive Speeds Statistics

Daniel had doubtless never traveled faster than on horseback. And probably his most common speed was his walking pace. In fact, this was the speed of all men until about mid-19th century.

With the invention of steam engines and electric power, men were sent down roads and rivers at speeds of 5 to 19 miles per hour. Then Henry Ford invented the internal combustion engine and speeds to 25, 35, even 70 miles per hour were posted.

Today, cars can travel at a maximum

of 600 mph, planes 2,000, and space ships 24,000.

　　　　　　　　　　　　　—Tim LaHaye

494　Around-The-World Speeds

A jet can fly around the world in 24 hours. A spacecraft can orbit the world in 80 minutes. And in less than one second, a radio message can reach the ends of the earth.

And if "anti-gravity" can be discovered, man will be traveling at the speed of light, or 7½ times around the world per second.

STEWARDSHIP

495　In Business For God

A businessman has no business being in business just to make money. Every businessman automatically is in danger of making money his god. Whenever he makes a decision in favour of his business as opposed to the Lord Jesus Christ, he has made money his god, for the moment, at least. He is favouring mammon, and his priorities are mixed.

It is impossible to overemphasize the importance of right priorities, especially in the business world, though these priorities apply to the life of every believer.

Advice not to mix Christianity and business is heresy of the worst kind. A man's business, whatever it might be, ought to be an integrated and integral part of his Christianity. It either complements or opposes his spiritual stance.

　　　　　　　　　　　　—Walt Meloon

496　$10 To Members

Last September 12 David McClure, pastor of the Unity Church, Spokane, WA, told the members of his congregation they could take a $10 bill from the church funds, turn their talents to increasing the

sum, and then bring back the results in 50 days.

Church members took about $3,500.

On November 14 a special collection was taken. The total was $10,207.24.

Commented Mr. McClure: "There were a few members who thought we'd be doing well just to get our money back on this thing. It was a step in faith, and it proved one of the principles of faith: the power of putting your faith and trust in people."

　　　　　　　　—Prairie Overcomer

497　Long Walk Included

One of my favorite stories is about a missionary teaching in Africa. Before Christmas, he had been telling his native students how Christians, as an expression of their joy, gave each other presents on Christ's birthday.

On Christmas morning, one of the natives brought the missionary a seashell of lustrous beauty. When asked where he had discovered such an extraordinary shell, the native said he had walked many miles to a certain bay, the only spot where such shells could be found.

"I think it was wonderful of you to travel so far to get this lovely gift for me," the teacher exclaimed.

His eyes brightening, the native replied, "Long walk, part of gift."

　　　　　　　　　—Gerald H. Bath

SUNDAY

498　The Wrong Day?

"You see, God, it's like this: We could attend Church more faithfully if your day came to some other time. You have chosen a day that comes at the end of a hard week, and we're all tired out. Not only that, but it's day following Saturday night, and Saturday night is one time when we feel that we should go out and enjoy ourselves. Often it is after midnight when we reach home, and it is almost impossible to get up on Sunday morning. And you must realize that you have picked the very day on which the morning paper takes the longest to read—the day when the biggest meal of the week must be prepared. We'd like to go to church, and know that we should; but you have just chosen the wrong day."

— *Twentieth Century Christian*

499 Courageous Football Team

The most courageous football team in American history has to be the University of Sewannee squad of 1899 that remained undefeated with five games to go in six days against five of the most powerful teams in the country in five different cities many miles apart. This was long before the time when football teams would fly in chartered jet aircraft.

They defeated Texas University 12-0 in the first game. The next day, after traveling by horse and wagon and with little rest, they dumped Texas A & M 32-0.

After another long ride by wagon, Sewannee played its third consecutive game in three days against Tulane University and won 23-0.

The fourth day was Sunday. The squad took time off for prayer and rest. The next day they downed undefeated Louisiana State University 34-0, then the following day beat Mississippi State 12-0.

The five powerhouses couldn't score against Sewannee, which played with only 11 men and no substitutes.

— James C. Hefley

500 Epigram

●Our great-grandfathers called it the holy Sabbath; our grandfathers, the Sabbath; our fathers, Sunday; but today we call it the week-end.

— *Wesleyan Methodist*

●Millions long for immortality who do not know what to do with themselves on a rainy Sunday afternoon.

— Susan Ertz

●"A world without a Sabbath would be like a man without a smile, like a summer without flowers, and like a homestead without a garden. It is the joyous day of the week." — Henry Ward Beecher

●I can never hope to destroy Christianity until I first destroy the Christian Sabbath.   — Voltaire

●Tell me what the young men of England are doing on Sunday, and I will tell you what the future of England will be.
— Gladstone

●Jesus spoke about the ox in the ditch on the Sabbath. But if your ox gets in the ditch every Sabbath, you should either get rid of the ox or fill up the ditch."
— Billy Graham

SUNDAY SCHOOL

501 Origin Of Sunday School

The Sunday School was not originated by famous theologians. In 1780, businessman Robert Raikes saw dirty children on Sunday afternoon with their favorite activity: fist fights. Sunday afternoon was the only free day from hard work then.

Mr. Raikes established the first Sunday School with the dirty small children, which was promptly dubbed "Raikes Regiment" and "Billy Wild Goose." For those who came, he gave pennies; teachers were hired at 25¢ per Sunday. Later, John Wesley was the first to suggest the elimination of payment, and the movement spread.

502 World's Largest Sunday School

A new world record Sunday School attendance of 23,024 was set by the First Baptist Church of Hammond, Indiana. It had already earned the title of "The

World's Largest Sunday School" previously. The average attendance for the fall and winter months of 1973 had been 13,000.

503 Perfect Attendance Records

Who holds the world record for perfect Sunday School attendance?

First there was Mrs. Harry C. Morgan of Greene Street Presbyterian Church, Augusta, Georgia, who reached her 45th year of perfect Sunday School attendance in 1959—a total of 2340 consecutive Sundays!

Then there is Miss Jennie C. Powers of Philadelphia, Pa., who attended without absence for 56 years and four months—a total of 2938 Sundays.

But according to *Guinness Book of Records*, it is Roland E. Daab of Columbia, Illinois who beats the record. On May 23, 1976, he attended his 3,000th consecutive Sunday School session—an unbroken period of over 57 years.

504 What's The Matter With Mrs. Craig?

The following news items appeared in the *Nashville Banner*, June 19, 1956:

PORTER, Okla. (AP)—Mrs. Ella Craig, age 81, hasn't missed Sunday School attendance in 1,040 Sundays—a perfect record for 20 years.

1. Doesn't Mrs. Craig ever have company on Sunday to keep her away from church?

2. Doesn't she ever go anywhere on Saturday night and get up tired on Sunday morning?

3. Doesn't she ever have headaches, colds, nervous spells, tired feelings, poor breakfast, sudden calls out of town, business trips, Sunday picnics, or any trouble of any kind?

4. Doesn't she have any friends at all—friends who invite her to a week end trip to the sea shore or mountains?

5. Doesn't she ever sleep late on Sunday morning?

6. Doesn't it ever rain or snow on Sunday mornings?

7. Doesn't she ever get her feelings hurt by somebody in church?

8. Doesn't she ever get mad at the preacher or Sunday School teacher?

9. Doesn't she have a radio or television so she can listen to "some mighty good sermons from out of town?"

What's the matter with Mrs. Craig?

505 Compared With TV Time

The average US child will, by age 65, have spent 9 years of 24-hour sitting in front of a TV set. But if he goes to Sunday School every Sunday during those years, he will have spent only 4 months studying the Bible.

506 Story Of Dillinger

Somewhere I read of a rough boy who attended a Sunday School and made it tough for every teacher he had. Finally, after a consultation with the teachers, the Superintendent led him to the door one Sunday with this curt dismissal: "There's the street. Go, and never come back to this Sunday School!"

He never came back, but they heard from him again! He began a career of crime and bloodshed that perhaps has never been equalled in modern times. Finally, before a theater entrance in Chicago one evening, his body was riddled with bullets.

In one of the Chicago papers a most unusual picture appeared—only the feet of the dead desperado showed. The caption under the picture was brief: "These are the feet of John Dillinger!" The editorial comment was heartsearching: "Who knows where these feet might have gone if someone had guided them aright?"

Little do we realize how much our present attitudes and actions may mold the future and determine the destiny of the boy or girl who shares our home or lives on our street. What a terrible price we pay for neglect!

507 Epigram
● "WANTED: Teacher. Must have the

Sunday School

wisdom of Solomon, patience of Job, and the courage of David."

That's the ad I'd run if I wanted to find the ideal Sunday School teacher!

—Dick VanDyke

T

TEARS

508 When Vassar Sat On Doorsteps

Uncle John Vassar, "one of the greatest soul-winners of his century," was going from door to door distributing tracts and speaking with people as opportunity came. An Irish woman heard of this strange man who was entering the houses of the town without introduction, and said, "If he comes to my door he shall not be kindly treated."

The next day, with no knowledge of this threat, he rang her bell. When she recognized him she slammed the door in his face. Nothing daunted, he sat upon the doorstep and sang:

"But drops of grief can ne'er repay
The debt of love I owe;
Here, Lord I give myself away;
'Tis all that I can do."

A few weeks later this woman sought admission to a church. As she made her confession before the Elders she could only say between her sobs, "'Twas those drops of grief. They burned themselves into my heart."

—George L. Rulison

509 "Give Me Back My Tears"

One of the mightiest soul winners I ever knew was Colonel Clark of Chicago. He would work at his business six days every week. And every night in the week the year around five or six hundred men would gather together in that mission hall. It was a motly crowd: drunkards, thieves, pickpocketers, gamblers and everything that was hopeless. I used to go and hear Colonel Clark talk, and he seemed to me one of the dullest talkers I have ever heard in my life. He would ramble along and yet these five or six hundred men would lean over and listen spellbound while Colonel Clark talked in his prosy way.

Some of the greatest preachers in Chicago used to go down to help Colonel Clark, but the men would not listen to them as they did to Colonel Clark. When he was speaking they would lean over and listen and be converted by the score. I could not understand it. I studied it and wondered what the secret of it was. Why did these men listen with such interest, and why were they so greatly moved by such prosy talking?

I found the secret. It was because they knew that Colonel Clark loved them, and nothing conquers like love. The tears

146

were very near the surface with Colonel Clark. Once in the early days of the mission, when he had been weeping a great deal over these men, he got ashamed of his tears. He steeled his heart and tried to stop his crying, and succeeded, but lost his power. He saw that his power was gone and he went to God and prayed. "Oh, God, give me back my tears," and God gave him back his tears, and gave him wonderful power, marvelous power over these men.

If we would see the seed that we sow bring an abundant harvest, we must water it with our tears. "He that goeth forth and weepeth, bearing precious seed, shall doubtless come again with rejoicing, bringing in his sheaves with him."

—R. A. Torrey

510 John R. Rice's Experience

When I first began preaching, I remember how I wept from the beginning to the end of my sermons. I was embarrassed of it. This was wholly unlike the college debating, the commencement addresses and other public speaking which I had been accustomed to doing. The tears flowed down my cheeks almost continually, and I was so broken up that sometimes I could scarcely talk. Then I grew ashamed of my tears and longed to speak more logically. As I recall, I asked the Lord to give me better control of myself as I preached.

My tears soon vanished and I found I had only the dry husk of preaching left. Then I begged God to give me again the broken heart, the concern, even if it meant tears in public and a trembling voice. I feel the same need today. We preachers ought to cry out like Jeremiah, "Oh, that my head were waters, and mine eyes a fountain of tears, that I might weep day and night for the slain of the daughter of my people!" (Jer. 9:1)

—John R. Rice

TEMPTATION

511 Our Weakest Moments

Temptation often comes not at our strongest, but our weakest moments. When we are at the limit of our patience, love, etc. we are tempted to be unChristian, beware. Jesus' temptation began *after* 40 days of fasting.

People usually are more impressed when they see us act under pressure. One weak act may spoil a whole lifetime of witness.

512 Gleam In Own Eye?

Letter to Dear Abby: "Since I am pastor with 43 years' experience, I'd like to offer this suggestion to the inexperienced young minister who didn't know how to handle a very bold woman in his congregation who had designs on him.

"Whenever I noticed a romantic twinkle in the eye of a woman in my congregation, I always checked to make sure it wasn't caused by a reflection from the gleam in my own. The Rev. Walter Cowen."

513 Epigram

●Temptation, if not resisted, soon becomes necessity.

●Watch out for temptation—the more you see of it the better it looks!

●If you value your corn, pluck out the grass.   —Malay Proverb

●Few speed records are broken when people run from temptation.

—E.C. Mckenzie

●One-half the trouble of this life can be traced to saying yes too quick, and not saying no soon enough.   —Josh Billings

●It is easier to suppress the first desire than to satisfy all that follow it.

—Franklin

●He that labors is tempted by one devil; he that is idle, by a thousand.

—Italian Proverb

THANKFULNESS

514 Repeated Thanks Not Copyrightable

One item sent in for copyright at the Library of Congress was a book written by a whimsical Texas businessman, who intended to hand out copies to his customers and friends. Its title was *A Million Thanks*, and it consisted of the word "thanks" repeated one million times.

"No thanks," replied the Library, declining to register it because a single word is not copyrightable.

515 Thank God For God

"The roar of the world is in my ears.
Thank God for the roar of the world;
Thank God for the mighty tide of fears
Against me always hurled.

"Thank God for the bitter and ceaseless strife,
And the sting of his chastening rod.
Thank God for the strees and pain of life,
And O, thank God for God!"

—Selected

516 Washington's Proclamation

WHEREAS, It is the duty of all nations to acknowledge the providence of Almighty God, to obey His will, to be grateful for His benefits, and humbly to implore His protection and favor;

WHEREAS, Both the house of Congress have, by their joint committee, requested me "to recommend to the people of the United States a day of public thanksgiving and prayer, to be observed by acknowledging with grateful hearts the many and signal favors of Almighty God, especially by affording them an opportunity peaceably to establish a form of government for their safety and happiness"!

Now, therefore, I do recommend next, to be devoted by the people of the states to the service of that great and glorious being, who is the beneficent Author of all the good that was, that is, or that will be, that we may then all unite in rendering unto Him our sincere and humble thanks for His kind care and protection of the people of this country.

—George Washington

TIME

517 Time Spent In 70-Year Life

If one lives to be 70 years of age and is the average person, he spends:
—20 years sleeping
—20 years working
—6 years eating
—7 years playing
—5 years dressing
—1 year on the telephone
—2½years smoking
—2½years in bed
—3 years waiting for somebody
—5 months tying shoes
—2½years for other things
  (incl. 1½year in church)

518 Lifetime In Minutes

Dr. Leslie Weatherhead, in his book, *Time for God* has a mathematically calculated schedule which compares a lifetime of "three score years and ten" with the hours of a single day from seven in the morning to eleven at night.

"If your age is:
15, the time is 10:25 a.m.
20, the time is 11:34 a.m.
25, the time is 12:42 p.m.
30, the time is 1:51 p.m.
35, the time is 3:00 p.m.
40, the time is 4:08 p.m.

45, the time is   5:16 p.m.
50, the time is   6:25 p.m.
55, the time is   7:34 p.m.
60, the time is   8:42 p.m.
65, the time is   9:51 p.m.
70, the time is 11:00 p.m."

519 "A New Leaf"

He came to my desk with quivering
    lip—
  The lesson was done.
"Dear Teacher, I want a new leaf,"
    he said,
  "I have spoiled this one."

I took the old leaf, stained and blotted,
  And gave him a new one all
    unspotted,
And into his sad eyes smiled,
  "Do better, now, my child."

I went to the throne with a quivering
    soul—
  The old year was done.
"Dear Father, hast Thou a new leaf
    for me?
  I have spoiled this one."

He took the old leaf, stained and
    blotted,
  And gave me a new one all
    unspotted,
And into my sad heart smiled,
  "Do better, now, my child."
           —Kathleen Wheeler

520 Another Year Is Dawning

Another year is dawning,
Dear Master, let it be,
In working, or in waiting,
Another year with Thee.

Another year of mercies,
Of faithfulness and grace;
Another year of gladness
In the shining of Thy face.

Another year of progress,
Another year of praise,

Another year of proving
Thy presence all the days.

Another year of service,
Of witness of Thy love,
Another year of training
For holier work above.

Another year is dawning,
Dear Master, let it be
On earth, or else in heaven
Another year for Thee.
          —Francis Ridley Havergal

521 Epigram

●No matter what a man's past may
have been, his future is spotless.
          —John R. Rice

TRAVEL

522 200 Million Yearly

International tourism is a huge business—it involves 200 million people traveling outside their own countries every
year throughout the world. This mass of
tourists, nearly equal to the population of
the entire United States, spends $24 bil-
lion a year abroad, not including air fares.

523 Traveling People

Stand on any busy street corner, or
expressway, and watch the cars go by. Air
terminals are crowded with passengers,
the air lanes are filled with planes. Many
people travel further now on a weekend
than their fathers did in a lifetime.

524 Epigram

●One who travels thoughtfully adds
another dimension to life.

●In this jet era of tremendous speed,
you can now have early breakfast in New
York and fly to Los Angeles in time to find
nobody up.   —*Woman's Day*

●A tourist in Switzerland was taken

by a local guide on a mountain climb. At one point the guide disturbed his client by urging: "Be careful not to fall here because it is very dangerous. But if you do fall, remember to look to the right—the view is the best for miles around."
— *Tit-Bits*

●Every year it takes less time to fly across the ocean and longer to drive to the office. — *Saturday Evening Post*

●Monty Woolley slipped on the stairs of the Times Square subway station one rainy night when there were no taxis to be had. Halfway down, he bumped into a stout lady, who toppled against him and landed on his lap at the stairs. Woolley tapped her on the shoulder and pointed out, "Madam, I'm sorry, but this is as far as I go."

●How long should a vacation be? Just long enough for the boss to miss you, but not long enough for him to discover that he can get along without you.

TRIVIALITIES

525 Ivy League Trivia Contest

Over 1,000 college-age students poured into Columbia University's Macmillan Theater to watch the Second Annual Ivy League Trivia Contest.

The Ivy League contest is the biggest of many contests in which thousands of players compete to see who knows the most about things which matter the least.

Pennsylvania remembered the 1946 song: "Use Ajax, bumm, bumm, the foaming cleanser." Yale recalled that Harpo Marx sold "tootsi-frootsi" ice cream. But Princeton won the contest by naming Rosemary Clooney as the singer of "Come On-a My House" and identifying El Fago Baca as the Walt Disney character with nine lives. The winning trophy was a green 49¢ mixing bowl.

This could happen in affluent, indifferent America while millions of illiterates in other lands scavenge for scraps of food by day and toss fitfully in cardboard shelters by night.

526 Typing To 1,000,000

Between 1968 and 1974, Mrs. Marva Drew of Waterloo, Iowa typed from 1 to 1,000,000 on a manual typewriter. When asked why, she replied, "But I love to type." She used 2,473 pages for that feat of triviality.

527 Two Russian Guards On Lawn

This is a story about Russia in the days of the Czars. In the park of St. Petersburg's Winter Palace there was a beautiful lawn, on that lawn a bench, and next to that bench, two guards. Every three hours the guards were changed. No one knew why. One day an ambitious young lieutenant was put in charge of the Palace Guard. He started wondering, and asking questions. In the end, he found a cobwebby little old man, the Palace historian.

"Yes," the old man said, "I remember. During the reign of Peter the Great, 200 years ago, the bench got a fresh coat of paint. The Czar was afraid that the ladies in waiting might get paint on their dresses. So he ordered one guard to watch the bench. The order was never rescinded. Then in 1908, all the guards of the Palace were doubled for fear of a revolution. So the bench has had two guards ever since."

— Maxwell Droke

528 Epigram

●A good memory is one trained to forget the trivial. — Clifton Fadiman

●The man who fiddles around seldom gets to lead the orchestra.
— E.C. Mckenzie

●The secret of John Wesley's power was his kingly neglect of trifles as he mastered the important thing—the

preaching of the gospel.
—Bishop Gerald Kenedy

TROUBLES-BLESSINGS

529 "Changing Pastures"

I saw the other day a painting of a large boat laden with cattle that were being ferried across an angry, swollen river in time of storm. The artist had so cleverly pictured the dark, threatening clouds and the play of the treacherous, jagged lightning that I immediately concluded that the freight of poor, dumb cattle was marked for destruction. But the title of the picture was simply, "Changing Pastures."
—Harold P. Barker

530 "Home, Sweet Home"

If he had not been a homeless wanderer, probably John Howard Payne never would have voiced the homesickness of humanity in his tender lyric, "Home, Sweet Home."
—Cut Gems

531 The Girl's Giggle

E. Stanley Jones' mind went blank when he started to preach his first sermon in Baltimore, and as he was about to sit down in dismay, the giggle of a girl put fire into him.

532 Forced To Oatmeal Diet

A certain missionary found herself seriously ill in the outpost where the Lord had stationed her. To add to her sorrow her check had not arrived and she was forced day after day to do without the good food she needed and to live on a miserable diet of oatmeal and canned milk. In spite of everything, the lady missionary got better, and after 30 days of steady oat meal diet, She finally got her check and was able to get something different on the table.

During her illness she had "a little sneaking suspicion" that the Lord was not doing her right. When furlough time came, she told of her great trial to an eager audience. At the close of the meeting, a kindly doctor inquired as to the nature of her ailment. On hearing what the digestional malfunction was, he said, "Well, if your check had arrived, you would not be here talking to me today. And the diet we always prescribe for that trouble is a 30-day oatmeal diet."
—Christian Victory

533 Epigram

●The brook would lose its song if we removed the rocks.

●The triumph song of life would lose its melody without its minor keys.
—Sunshine

●What sea has no waves? What land has no rain?

●The existence of sea means the existence of pirates. —Malay Proverbs

●There is no education like adversity.
—Benjamin Disraeli

●Difficulties strengthen the mind as labour does the body. —Seneca

●Adversity makes men, and prosperity makes monsters.
—Victor Hugo

●Even a misfortune may prove useful in three years. —Japanese Proverb

●The important thing about a problem is not its solution, but the strength we gain in finding the solution.

●I saw a star, I reached for it, I missed. So I accepted the sky.

●There was never a picture painted,
    There was never a poem sung,
    But the soul of the artist fainted,
    And the poet's heart was wrung.

●The ancients used an interesting little instrument, called the *tribulum*, to beat grain to divide the chaff from the wheat. The word "tribulation" comes from this word. Tribulations truly separate the chaff from the wheat in human character.

TRUST

---

534 Trust And OK

I rather like the small boy's version of the hymn, "Trust and Obey," when he said that at Sunday school they had been singing "Trust and O. K." Good! Everything must be O. K. if the life has been committed to His precious keeping. There is no other way.

—Expositor

535 Middle Verse Of Bible

This text is found in a Psalm which is signalized by the fact that it contains the middle verse of the Bible, namely, "It is better to trust in the Lord than to put confidence in man." (Ps. 118:9).

536 Moody's Favorite Verse

Dwight L. Moody's favorite verse was Isaiah 12:2: "I will trust, and not be afraid." He used to say: "You can travel first class or second class to heaven. Second class is, 'What time I am afraid, I will trust.'" First class is, 'I will trust, and not be afraid.'" That is the better way. Why not buy a first-class ticket?

537 Epigram

●The man who trust men will make fewer mistakes than he who distrusts them.

●A radio announcer once asked Leo Durocher, manager of the New York Giants, "Barring the unforeseen, Leo will your club get the pennant?" Back came Durocher's reply, "There ain't gonna be no unforeseen."

V

VANITIES

538 Medals For Sale

Nothing better illustrates the declaration of the apostle that "all the glory of man is the flower of the field" than the display in a pawnshop of the following list of medals for sale:

French Croix de Guerre	$2.00
American Distinguished Service Medal	10.00
Belgian Croix de Guerre	2.00
French Legion d' Honneur	12.00
German Iron Cross	1.00
Mons Star (1914)	1.00
Mons Star (1915)	.50
Italian War Cross	3.00

If poverty has compelled the living to thus part with this badge of a nation's honor, only a deep sense of sacrificial service rendered can neutralize the bitterness that almost necessarily lurk in the heart.

539 Allergic Queen

Olympia, Washington. (UPI) — Miss Becky Alexander, 18, the 1973 Washington Wheat Queen, had an embarrassing confession to make before the State Senate — she's allergic to wheat.

"I 'm probably the only wheat queen in history who is allergic to wheat," she told the lawmakers. She immediately put down a sheaf of what she had been carrying.

540 "Here Lies (Napoleon)"

The body of Napoleon I, exhumed from its plain wooden casket in October, 1840, (19 years after his death) had not decomposed although his leather boots had rotten off.

The stone above his tomb on St. Helena had on it only the word "CI-GIT"- or "HERE LIES!" He had requested a simple burial, that his ashes be spread on the banks of the Seine near the people he loved ... But his final resting place was the Ornate Hotel des Invalides.

541 Remains Of "Seven Wonders"

About all that remains of the so called "Seven Wonders" of the ancient world are as follows:

The only remains of the tomb of Mausolus, built in 350 B.C., are now exhibited in the British Museum.

The Temple of Artemis at Ephesus,

once the center of the fertility cult of Diana, was probably destroyed in A.D. 262 by the Goths. This was about 200 years after the city was visited by Paul.

The Hanging Gardens of Babylon grow no more. They adorned one of the world's spectacular cities during the reign of Nebuchadnezzar. Babylon's ruins have been found on the Euphrates River, about fifty-five miles south of modern Baghdad.

The magnificent statue of Zeus once stood forty-feet high in the city of Olympus where the Olympian games were held every four years. During Byzantine times plunderers dragged off and burned the huge statue.

King Ptolemy's famous lighthouse near Alexandria, Egypt, was built 200 feet square at the base. It crumpled during a fourteenth-century earthquake.

The Colossus of Rhodes met the same fate in 224 B.C. It was originally a giant 100-foot statue of Apollo that spanned the harbon on the isle of Rhodes.

Only the pyramids, built before the time of Moses, have survived the ravages of time. They were built as tombs for the pharaohs who fully expected to be revived after death.

— Aames C. Hefley

542 Epigram

●Those who live must die, those who meet must part.   — Japanese Proverb

●Meeting is the beginning of parting.
— Japanese Proverbs

●Youth is a blunder; manhood a struggle; old age a regret.
— Benjamin Disraeli

●Every day the world turns over on someone who had just been sitting on top of it.

●Napoleon summarized his own fading fame in a single sentence: "I am doing now what will fill thousands of volumes in this generation; in the next, one volume will contain it all; in the third, a paragraph; in the fourth, a single line."

VISION

543 A Crying Boy In Glasgow

The story is told of William C. Burns, the man who mightily blessed Hudson Taylor and Murray McCheyne, of how when he was only a boy of seventeen he visited the city of Glasgow with his mother for the first time in his life. The mother suddenly lost her boy in the crowd and after many anxious moments discovered him in an alley with his head buried in his hands, sobbing with a broken heart.

"What ails you, lad?" asked the Scottish mother. "Oh, Mither, Mither," said the country boy, "the thud of these Christless feet on the way to hell breaks my heart." One can understand how he grew up to be the mighty revivalist of Scotland and China.

— Alliance Weekly

544 Dannaker Refuses Napoleon's Request

Dannaker, the German sculptor, worked for two years on a statue of Christ. It looked finished and perfect to him.

To test it he called into the studio a little girl, and pointing to the statue, asked "Who is that?"

She replied promptly, "A great man."

He turned away disheartened, knowing that he had failed.

But he took his chisel and began anew. For six more long years he toiled, and inviting another little girl into his workshop, he stood her before the figure and said, "Who is that?"

She looked up at it for a moment and the tears began to gather in her eyes as she folded her hands across her breast and said, "Suffer the little children to come unto me."

It was enough. Dannaker knew that his task was done. Then the sculptor confessed that during the weary days of those six years, the Christ had come and revealed Himself to him. He had only transferred to the marble the vision he had seen.

Sometime later Napoleon Bonaparte requested him to make a statue of Venus for the Louvre. But he refused. "A man," he said, "who had *seen Christ* can never employ his gifts in carving a pagan goddess. My art is henceforth a consecrated thing."

　　　　　　　　　　— *The Presbyterian*

545 "More Beyond"

Spain once held both sides of the Mediterranean at the Straits of Gibraltar. So highly did she value her possessions, that she stamped on her coin the two Pillars of Hercules (as the promontories of rock were called); and on a scroll thrown over these were the words, "ne plus ultra",—"no more beyond."

But one day a bold spirit sailed far beyond these pillars, and found a new world of beauty. Then Spain, wisely convinced of ignorance, struck the word "ne" from the coin, and left "plus ultra",— "more beyond."

　　　　　　　　　　　　　— Foster

546 Epigram

●The poorest man is not he who is without a cent, but he who is without a dream.　　— *Pennsylvania School Journal*

●It is reported that Moody's farewell words to his sons as he lay upon his deathbed were. "If God be your partner, make your plans large."

●To the Israelites, Goliath is "too big to hit"; but to little David, he is "too big to miss."

●There is a vast difference between a person with a vision and a visionary person. The person with a vision talks little but does much. The person who is visionary talks much but does nothing.

●The albatross has the widest wing span of all birds in relation to body-size. It occurs to me that some people have large wing spreads, in relation to body size, which enables them to fly on and on.

　　　　　　　　　— M. Dale Baughman

WAR

547 Thirteen-To-One Rate Of Peace

On the basis of the computation in the *Moscow Gazette*, Gustave Valbert in his day could report that "from the year 1496 BC to AD, 1861 in 3,358 years there were 227 years of peace and 3,130 years of war, or 13 years of war to every year of peace. Within the last 3 centuries, there have been 286 wars in Europe. He added that from the year 1500 BC to AD, 1860 more than 8,000 treaties of peace, meant to remain in force forever, were concluded. The average time they remained in force was 2 years.

548 But The War Happened

According to Jamie Portman of *The Calgary Herald*. "Back in 1960, a U.S. military research team was studying the ways and means of avoiding the outbreak of another major war.

"In the course of its research, the team fed a computer with all the date pertaining to the First World War. The computer responded with the assertion that the First World War was an impossibility, that it never really happened, that blun-ders and casualties of such magnitude could only be the stuff of fictional conjecture, not of hard reality.

"But the First World War did happen. It cost an estimated $105 billion to stage, and it killed an estimated 10 million human beings. And it's recalled today through the mists of nostalgia, tempered with an unmistakable sense of outrage, that the 1914-18 war—and the folly and carnage which it represented—really did take place."

549 How Do Wars Begin?

A boy once asked, "Dad, how do wars begin?" "Well, take the First World War," said his father. "That got started when Germany invaded Belgium." Immediately his wife interrupted him. "Tell the boy the truth. It began because somebody was murdered." The husband drew himself up with an air of superiority and snapped back, "Are you answering the question or am I?"

Turning her back upon him in a huff, the wife walked out of the room and slammed the door as hard as she could. When the dishes stopped rattling in the cupboard, an uneasy silence followed, broken at length by the son. "Daddy, you don't have to tell me how wars begin; *I know now!"*

550 Epigram

●It has been said that "the only thing history teaches us is that history teaches us nothing."

●Mankind must put an end to war or war will put an end to mankind.

—John F. Kennedy

●On May 12, 1962, General MacArthur spoke to the graduating class at West Point. In his speech the General quoted Plato to the effect that "only the dead have seen the end of war."

WATCHFULNESS

551 If Next Sunday

If Christ should come next Sunday,
    And it may be that He will,
Would the thing that I'll be doing
    Set the Master's heart athrill?

If the Christ should come next Sunday
    Would he find me loyal, true,
In my place with my influence
    Doing what He'd have me do?

If the Christ should come next Sunday,
    Let's suppose He came at ten,
Would He hear me answer "present"
    In the class I should attend?

If the Christ should come next Sunday,
    If He came just at eleven,
Would He find me in His service,
    Singing praises unto heaven?

—Selected

552 Boatman's Lone Star

An artist once drew a picture. It represented a night-scene. A solitary man is rowing a little skiff across a lake; the wind is high and stormy, the billows, white and crested, rage around the frail bark; and not a star, save one, shines through the dark and angry sky above. But upon that lone star the voyager fixes his eye, and keep rowing away—on, on, on through the mid-night storm. Written beneath the picture were these words, "If I lose that I'm lost!"

—Denton

553 Pompeii's Sentinel

When Pompeii was destroyed by the eruption of Mt. Vesuvius there were many persons buried in the ruins who were afterward found in very different positions.

There were some found in deep vaults, as if they had gone there for security. There were some found in lofty chambers. But where did they find the Roman sentinel?

They found him standing at the city gate where he had been placed by the captain, with his hands still grasping the weapon. There, while the earth shook beneath him; there, while the floods of ashes and cinders overwhelmed him, he had stood at his post; and there, after a thousand years, he was found.

So let Christians stand by their duty in the post at which their Captain places them.

—*Gospel Trumpet*

554 Expecting A Different "Johnson"

During President Johnson's administration, the First Lady flew to Cleveland one day, and then decided to return to Washington by automobile. Reservations were made for the party of 20 to eat lunch en route at one of the Howard Johnson restaurants. During lunch, one of the waitresses serving the group was extremely nervous. Afterward, Press Secretary Liz Carpenter thanked the girl and said she could understand her nervousness: "It isn't every day that you serve Mrs. Lyndon Johnson."

"Mrs. Lyndon Johnson!" the waitress exclaimed. "I thought it was Mrs. Howard Johnson."

—Vivian Vance

555 Epigram
●The term "argus-eyed" means being extraordinarily watchful. Thus, an argus-eyed committee may watch the counting of the money or the ballots. Argus, a monster in Greek mythology, had one hundred eyes, only two of which were said to sleep at once.

●The German eagle had its head turned to our left hand, and the Roman eagle to our right hand. When Charlemagne was made "Kaiser of the Holy Roman Empire," he joined the two heads together, one looking east and the other west. —Brewer

●"So you use three pairs of glasses, Professor?" "Yes, one pair for long sight, one pair for short sight, and the third to look for the other two." —The Lookout

WILL OF GOD

556 A Definition
You ask: "What is the will of God?"
Well, here's the answer true;
"The nearest thing, that should be done,
That he can do—through you!"

—E.C. Baird

557 Epigram
●An aged preacher prayed: "Oh, Lord, use me as Thou wilt—if only in an advisory capacity."

558 More Detailed Figure
The number of adherents in the world's principal religions are as follows:

Pagan	924 million
Roman Catholic	584 million
Muslim	455 million
Hindu	395 million
Protestant	224 million
Buddhist	161 million
Eastern Orthodox	142 million
Shintoist	67 million
Taoist	51 million
Jewish	13 million

WORLD CHURCH

559 World Council Of Churches
The World Council of Churches (WCC) held its first meeting in 1948. It is a fellowship of over 120 Protestant, Anglican, Orthodox and Old Catholic churches from some 90 countries throughout the world. Total membership: 400 million.

The first goal of the ecumenical movement spearheaded by the WCC is to bring all churches into one visible organization. The ultimate goal of the movement is to bring all relgions together. The WCC now holds dialogues on "peace" with representatives of 1.5 billion people on earth.

560 US Soldier In Hindu Headdress
The first U.S. soldier permitted to wear a Hindu headdress, Private Hari Nam Singh Elliott, 23, received honors of "best recruit" in his basic-training unit. He was allowed to keep his long red beard as well as his turban and to wear religious jewelry.

WORRY

561 When Birds Worry
When the birds begin to worry
And the lilies toil and spin,
And God's creatures all are anxious,
Then I also may begin.

For my Father sets their table,
Decks them out in garments fine,

And if He supplies their living,
Will He not provide for mine?

Just as noisy, common sparrows
Can be found most anywhere—
Unto some just worthless creatures,
If they perish who would care?

Yet our Heavenly Father numbers
Every creature great and small,
Caring even for the sparrows.
Marking when to earth they fall.

If His children's hairs are numbered,
Why should we be filled with fear?
He has promised all that's needful,
And in trouble to be near.
           —Anonymous

562 Nine Out Of Ten

There is no disputing the fact that, nine times out of ten, worrying about a thing does more damage to those who worry than the actual thing itself.

Modern medical research has proved that worry breaks down resistance to disease. More than that, it actually diseases the nervous system—particularly that of the digestive organs and of the heart. Add to this the toll in unhappiness of sleepless nights and days void of internal sunshine, and you have a glimpse of the work this monster does in destroying the effectiveness of the human body.

It is plain common sense that worry has no rightful place in the lives of most of us.

           —Ken Anderson

563 Epigram

●Ulcers is what you get from climbing mountains over mole hills.
          —*The Bible Friend*

●Worry is the advance interest you pay on troubles that seldom come.

●Worry, like a rocking chair, will give you something to do, but it won't get you anywhere.   —Vance Havner

●The beginning of anxiety is the end of faith. The beginning of true faith is the end of anxiety.   —George Muller

●An actor who's been visiting a psychiatrist for years says, "I must be the only guy who ever spent $10,000 on a couch—and still doesn't own it."

564 Epigram

●Don't spoil today by worrying about tomorrow. The hills flatten out when we come to them.   —*Phi Delta Kappan*

●The best way to forget all about your troubles is to wear a pair of tight shoes.
          —E.C. Mckenzie

●The little birds of the field have God for their caterer.   —Cervantes

●A good memory test: What were you worrying about this time last year?
          —Jack Key

●Blessed is the man who is too busy to worry in the daytime and too sleepy to worry at night.   —Phil Marquart

●A Negro woman lived to be ninety years old. When asked the secret of her longevity, she said, "When I works, I work hard, when I sits, I sits easy and when I worries, I go to sleep!"

WORSHIP

565 God Is Critic

"Most people think of the church as a drama," Dr. James Kennedy said, "with the minister as the chief actor, God as the prompter, and the laity as the critic. What is actually the case is that the congregation is the chief actor, the minister is the prompter, and God is the critic."

567 A Prescription For Worship

Enter the place of worship a little before the service begins. Enter expectantly. God has promised to meet you there. Whisper a prayer. When the first hymn is announced, open your hymnal to that place. If you cannot sing, follow the words. Bow your head and close your eyes during the prayer. As you give, pray that God will accept the gift. During the special music, be attentive and prayerful. When the minister preaches, pray for him and listen attentively. Be silent; expect to sing or to say "Amen!"

—*Evangelical Friend*

567 Queen Stands At "Messiah"

When Queen Victoria had just ascended her throne she went, as is the custom of Royalty, to hear "The Messiah" rendered. She had been instructed as to her conduct by those who knew, and was told that she must not rise when the others stood at the singing of the Hallelujah Chorus. When that magnificent chorus was being sung and the singers were shouting "Hallelujah! Hallelujah! Hallelujah! for the Lord God omnipotent reigneth," she sat with great difficulty.

It seemed as if she would rise in spite of the custom of kings and queens, but finally when they came to that part of the chorus where with a shout they proclaim Him King of Kings suddenly the young queen rose and stood with bowed head, as if she would take her own crown from off her head and cast it at His feet.

—J. Wilbur Chapman

WORSHIP, HOUSE OF

568 Little Girl Also Helped

When Milan Cathedral was finished, in

the vast throngs of people assembled to witness the dedication was a little girl who was heard to cry out in childish glee, as she pointed to the great building, "I helped to build that!" "What!" exclaimed one of the guards who was standing in brilliant uniform. "Show me what you did." "I carried the dinner pail for my father while he worked up yonder," she replied.

Her part, though humble, helped to complete the plans of the architect. In relating this story, Bishop Leonard makes this comment: "Our part in life may seem small, but it should bulk large in our thought when we remember that it is helping to complete the plan of the Divine Architect."

—*Christian Herald*

569 "Judas Iscariot!"

A minister riding a streetcar in N.Y. and passing a very nice church, sat next to a rider who said, "If these Christians would stop building fine churches and give their money to the poor, it would be much more to their credit." "I've heard of similar remark before" was minister's quiet reply. "By whom?" "Judas Iscariot."

570 Epigram

●Seen on a church bulletin board: "You aren't too bad to come in. You aren't too good to stay out."

—Indianapolis *Star*

YOUTH

571 Ages 15-19

VICTOR HUGO wrote a tragedy at 15, received three prizes at the Academy and the title of Master before he was 20. JOHN DE MEDECCI was cardinal at age 15. PASCAL wrote a great work at 16 and died at thirty-seven. RAPHAEL painted his wonderful works as a young man and died at thirty-seven.

CHATTERTON was already well-known at 18, and was unequalled among English poets at 21. TENNYSON wrote his first volume at 18. JOAN OF ARC did all her work and was burned at the stake at 19.

572 Ages 20-25

ROMULUS founded Rome at 20. GLADSTONE was in the Parliament in early manhood; while PITT and BOLINGBROKE were ministers almost before they were men.

CALVIN joined the Reformation at 21 and wrote the *Institutes* at 27, thus profoundly influencing the theological thought of later centuries.

ALEXANDER THE GREAT was a mere youth when he rolled back the Asiatic hordes that threatened to destroy European civilization almost at its birth, and conquered the world when he was 23.

ISAAC NEWTON was 24 when he formulated the Law of Gravity and made some of his greatest discoveries before 25. McCORMICK was 23 when he invented the reaper; and CHARLES DICKENS wrote his *Pickwick Papers* at 24 and *Oliver Twist* at 25.

573 Ages 25-26

MARTIN LUTHER was a triumphant reformer at 25, and started the Reformation at 30. FRANCIS OF ASSISI was 25 when he founded the Franciscan order; and JOHN OF AUSTRIA won the Battle of Lepanto—the greatest battle of modern times—at age 25. KEATS the divine singer was only a youth and died at 25.

WHITEFIELD were students with Wesley at Oxford and had made his influence felt throughout England before he was 24.

HANNIBAL commanded the Carthaginian forces at 26, and at that age BENJAMIN FRANKLIN wrote *Poor Richard's Almanac*.

574 Ages 27-29

At age 27, NAPOLEON conquered Italy and was recognized as the foremost commander of any age; PATRICK HENRY cried "Give me liberty or give me death!"; JOHN SMITH staked out a colonial empire in Virginia; and the evangelist SPURGEON built the great Metropolitan Tabernacle in London.

COLUMBUS had his plans all laid to find India when he was 28; and at that age, XAVIER teamed with Loyola to organize the Society of Jesuits. ROGER WILLIAMS was important enough to be banished as an heretic at 29.

575 Ages 30-37

IGNATIUS LOYOLA at age 30 founded the Society of Jesuits. And CORTES was 30 when he stood gazing at the golden treasures of Mexico.

BILLY GRAHAM was 31 at the time of his now-famous Los Angeles Crusade. HAMILTON was 32 when he was Secretary of the Treasury. And when MAURICE OF SAXONY died at age 32, all Europe owned him to be the profoundest statesman of his day.

BILLY SUNDAY left home plate for the pulpit at 33. JEFFERSON was also 33

when he drafted the Declaration of Inde- we know all the questions; at twenty we know all the answer.

● Remember what an old bishop said to a group of ministers: "None of you is infallible; not even the youngest of you."

● Our wisdom teeth are so called because they appear between the ages of seventeen and twenty-five, when it is assumed that their owners have reached a state of wisdom!   —David Jefferis

● The deepest loss of youth is the loss of the innocency and trust which belong to childhood.

576 Epigram

● Someone has figured out that the peak years of mental activity must be between the ages of four and twenty. At four pendence. And JOHN WESLEY began his real life's work at 35.

By age 37, BYRON, RAPHAEL and POE died after writing their names among the world's immortals. INNOCENT III, the greatest of the popes, was despot of Christendom at 37, and so was Pope FERDINAND of Aragon when Martin Luther robbed him of his greatest province at 35.

Z

ZEAL
---

577 Angel's Voice

We so often hear the expression "the voice of an angel" that I got to wondering what an angel would sound like. So I did some research, and discovered that an angel's voice sounds remarkably like a person saying, "Hurry up!"

Until the time I took over, research had been blocked because it was based on the delusion that the voice of an angel would always be beautiful. The words "Get up" are rarely beautiful, never less so than at 7 a.m. Yet that is what the angels always say when they talk to men, as reported in the Bible. I can't think of anything an angel ever said but "Get up and hurry!"

An angel comes to Peter in jail and says, "Rise quickly." An angel says to Gideon, "Arise and go in this thy might." An angel says to Elijah, "Arise and eat." An angel appears to Joseph in a dream, when Herod is slaughtering the infants, and says, "Go quickly." An angel appears to Philip and says, "Arise and go."

Really, the angels are monotonous talkers! They always say the same thing—"Arise, hurry!" But so is a fire bell monotonous.

It might be a good idea to allow an angel to occupy the pulpit on Sunday.
— *The Christian Century*

578 John Wesley

John Wesley averaged three sermons a day for fifty-four years preaching all-told more than 44,000 times. In doing this he traveled by horseback and carriage more than 200,000 miles, or about 5,000 miles a year.

His published words include a four-volume commentary on the whole Bible, a dictionary of the English language, a five-volume work on natural philosophy, a four-volume work on church history; histories of England and Rome; grammars on the Hebrew, Latin, Greek, French and English languages; three works on medicine, six volumes of church music; seven volumes of sermons and controversial papers. He also edited a library of fifty volumes known as "The Christian Library."

579 Zealous Preachers

John Wesley was denied the privilege of preaching from the pulpit in the church; but with true evangelistic fervor

163

took his father's tomb for a pulpit and preached to the people the great truths of full salvation. Whitefield loved field preaching. Returning from a tour he lighted a candle and went upstairs to retire, weary after the journey; but the people gathered in front of the house and filled the street; and there on the stairway with a lighted candle in his hand, he preached his last message, retired and was no more; for God took him.

John Knox, who cried out in his earnestness, "Give me Scotland or I die," carried with him this zeal to the close of his ministry. Often he would be supported by attendants in order to reach the pulpit; but when he arose to speak the divine passion so filled his soul that one of his friends said: "So mighty was he in his yearning that I thought he would break the pulpit into bits."

580 **Epigram**

●I am only an average man, but I work harder at it than the average man.

—Theodore Roosevelt

●When Thorwaldson was asked, "Which is your greatest statue," he replied, "The next one."

●Before you go to sleep, say to yourself, "I haven't reached by goal yet, whatever it is, and I'm going to be uncomfortable and in a degree unhappy until I do."   —Carl Sandburg

●Personal notice in the Flint, Mich., *Weekly Review:* "Barbershop quartet forming; need bass, baritone and tenor."

●Space scientist Dr. James Van Allen hasn't the two regular "In" and "Out" mail trays on his desk. Instead he has four, marked "Frantic," "Urgent," "Pressing" and "Overdue."

—Des Moines *Tribune*

INDEX

Index

170

S

133.18